—

# THIS IS
# WATERLOO
## REGION

DISCOVER THE FASCINATING FACTS, EXTRAORDINARY PEOPLE, UNIQUE
PLACES AND ENGAGING HISTORY OF THIS INNOVATIVE COMMUNITY

# J.M. Orend

# THIS IS WATERLOO REGION
## DISCOVER THE FASCINATING FACTS, EXTRAORDINARY PEOPLE, UNIQUE PLACES AND ENGAGING HISTORY OF THIS INNOVATIVE COMMUNITY

Published by Lomic Books

ISBN 978-09918039-1-0

Written by J.M. Orend, Copyright © 2014

Edited by Sam Orend, Paul Lomic and Marie Lomic

**Interior Images.** The author is grateful to the many individuals and organizations that granted permission to use their images in this book. Please refer to the Details section, on pages 71 and 72, for a comprehensive list of the interior images and their sources. The copyright of each image remains with the grantor who allowed the image to be used in this book, unless the image is in the public domain.

**Cover.** Design by JMO. Front cover images: Cityscape courtesy Matthew Smith; Grand River photograph by Chris Hill/Shutterstock.com; Clock Tower courtesy City of Kitchener Photo Galleries; Fall colours by JMO. Back cover images: Castle Kilbride courtesy Castle Kilbride National Historic Site; Waterloo Region Museum photo provided by Waterloo Region Museum, Region of Waterloo; Pioneer Settlers Memorial Tower courtesy of City of Kitchener Photo Galleries; Perimeter Institute by JMO; Waterloo Historic School House by JMO. The author is grateful to the above individuals and organizations that granted permission to use their images. The copyright of each image remains with the grantor who allowed the image to be used in this book.

We have worked hard to ensure the accuracy of the information in this book; however, we cannot be held liable for any errors, omissions or inconstancies. To check our information sources, please refer to page 72 of our Details section. We also have a Resources section on page 70 which provides a great starting point for further exploring Waterloo Region.

For more information on *This is Waterloo Region*, including ordering, please check out:

## www.ThisisWaterlooRegion.com

If you have comments or questions about the book please email: jmorend@thisiswaterlooregion.com.

# TABLE OF CONTENTS

# INTRODUCTION

This book will take you on a fascinating tour of Waterloo Region. First, we will walk through some basic information on the Region. Next, we will look at the Region's compelling history. In the following sections, we will explore the many activities and opportunities that Waterloo Region offers including: everyday life, education, business, arts, sports and health care. Completing the tour, we will look at the unique qualities of each city and township in the Region, and the glue that makes the Region feel like a community. Let's get started!

Map of Waterloo Region within Canada

## LOCATION

Waterloo Region is located in Ontario, Canada. Within Ontario, the Region is in the southwestern part of the province.

Waterloo Region is about an hour and ten minutes by car from Toronto, which is Canada's biggest city. The City of Toronto is located east of Waterloo Region, while Lake Huron is about an hour and a half by car to the west of Waterloo Region.

Map of Waterloo Region within Southern Ontario

In this map of Southern Ontario, you can see Waterloo Region is close to three great lakes: Lake Huron, Lake Ontario and Lake Erie.

## CITIES AND TOWNSHIPS

Waterloo Region is made up of three cities and four townships. The three cities are: City of Cambridge, City of Kitchener and City of Waterloo. The four townships are: Township of North Dumfries, Township of Wellesley, Township of Wilmot and the Township of Woolwich.

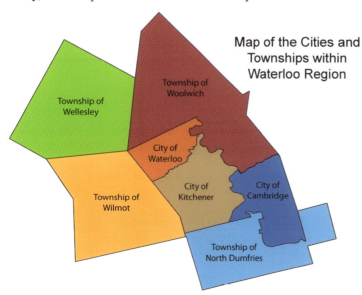

Map of the Cities and Townships within Waterloo Region

Waterloo Region's time zone is Eastern Standard Time, with Daylight Savings Time in the winter.

## SIZE OF REGION

The total area of Waterloo Region is 1,368.94 square kilometers.[1] The size of each of Waterloo Region's cities and townships are listed below.

| Location | Area[2] |
|---|---|
| City of Cambridge | 113.00 km[2] |
| City of Kitchener | 136.79 km[2] |
| City of Waterloo | 64.02 km[2] |
| Township of North Dumfries | 187.44 km[2] |
| Township of Wellesley | 277.79 km[2] |
| Township of Wilmot | 263.72 km[2] |
| Township of Woolwich | 326.17 km[2] |

# POPULATION

Waterloo Region has a population of approximately 559,000 people.[1] Below is a summary of the number of people living in each city and township in the Region.

| Location | Population[2] |
|---|---|
| City of Cambridge | 132,900 people |
| City of Kitchener | 232,000 people |
| City of Waterloo | 129,100 people* |
| Township of North Dumfries | 9,620 people |
| Township of Wellesley | 10,920 people |
| Township of Wilmot | 20,110 people |
| Township of Woolwich | 24,400 people |

* This number includes the students who move to the City of Waterloo to study at the local universities.

## Piece of History

The population of Waterloo Region in 1808 was only 425 people.[3]

However, the population grew steadily:[4]
- 1851 there were 26,537 people living in the Region.
- 1891 there were 50,464 people living in the Region.
- 1931 there were 89,852 people living in the Region.
- 1971 there were 253,221 people living in the Region.

The Region's population is expected to reach

# 729,000

people by 2031. Making it one of Canada's fastest growing communities.[5]

**4** The Region has the 4th biggest metropolitan population in Ontario, and the 10th biggest in Canada.[6]

# PHYSICAL GEOGRAPHY

Waterloo Region is located in the Mixedwoods Plains Ecozone that covers Southern Ontario. This ecozone is characterized by forests, rolling hills and plains. There are also many rivers, streams and lakes.

Within Waterloo Region, the soil is very productive which makes it conducive to farming. The Region also has extensive ground water aquifers made of gravel, rocks and sand that help store and supply some of Waterloo Region's drinking water.

The Grand River is an important source of drinking water in the Region. It was also one of the reasons settlers initially came to Waterloo Region.

To the left, you can see a crop of corn growing in the Region. The townships in Waterloo Region are filled with farms because of the high-quality soil in the Region.

Waterloo Region has an elevation of about 320 meters above mean sea level.

There are significant sand and gravel resources in the Region.

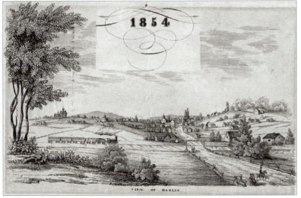

In this postcard drawing of the Town of Berlin, later called the City of Kitchener, you can see rolling hills. The rolling hills are now difficult to spot in the cities, but you can still see them in the townships.

Deciduous trees are trees that lose their leaves for the winter. These trees are common in the Region. In the fall, they make a beautiful sight when their leaves change colour from green to vibrant yellows, oranges and reds.

# EARLY SETTLERS
# ABORIGINAL PEOPLE

People have lived in Waterloo Region for a long time. In fact, experts estimate that people first inhabited Southern Ontario, including the area now known as Waterloo Region, 12,000 years ago. Through archeological research, we now have some idea of how people lived in the Region thousands of years ago.

This simple arrowhead was used to hunt. It is from the Paleo-Indian period (10,000 BC–7500 BC).

## PALEO-INDIAN AND ARCHAIC PERIODS

During the Paleo-Indian period (10,000 BC–7500 BC) Southern Ontario had a tundra-like environment, with small trees and cool temperatures. The main source of food for Aboriginal people was caribou and other animals. The animals were hunted with simple tools such as arrows. Hunting techniques and tools advanced during the Archaic Period (8,000 BC–800 BC). The tools were first made into a rough shape, and then ground and polished for hunting. As the climate warmed and more vegetation grew, Aboriginal people also collected nuts and berries for food.

These tools are from the Archaic period (8,000 BC–800 BC).

## WOODLAND PERIOD

There is archeological evidence of sophisticated farming methods and home building during the Woodland period (900 BC–1610 AD). During the Woodland period, the Aboriginal tribe known as the Neutral Nation lived in the Waterloo Region area. Pieces of longhouses and pottery used by the Neutral Nation have been found across the Region. Once the Neutral Nation dispersed, there were no permanent inhabitants in the Region until the Six Nations came to settle the land.

This piece of pottery is from the Woodland period (900 BC–1610 AD). Pottery is just one example of the increasing sophistication of tools that were made and used during the Woodland period.

To the left is an example of what a Neutral Nation longhouse may have looked liked 400 years ago.

Protected land in Waterloo Region called the Rare Charitable Research Reserve has evidence of over

# 130

Aboriginal sites.[1]

## HISTORIC SITES

There are many places in Waterloo Region where historic artifacts have been found. Some of these lands have been set aside as natural areas to conserve the Region's heritage and to provide residents places to connect with nature including: the Huron Natural Area in the City of Kitchener, and the Rare Charitable Research Reserve which is located in the City of Cambridge and the Township of North Dumfries.

This is a picture of the entrance to Huron Natural Area which celebrates the finding of archeological evidence of ten long houses dating back to 1500 AD.

6

# EARLY SETTLERS
# SIX NATIONS

The Six Nations was a coalition of six native tribes: the Mohawk, Oneida, Onondaga, Cayuga, Seneca and Tuscarora. The Six Nations were granted land in the area that is now Waterloo Region in 1784, by the British who administered Canadian lands during that time. The land grant was meant to reward the Six Nations for fighting on behalf of Britain to try to suppress the American Revolutionary War (1775–1783), and to compensate the Six Nations for the loss of their original homeland to the Americans because of this war.

Joseph Brant (1743–1807), also known as Thayendanegea, was considered a great Mohawk leader and warrior. He lead the Six Nations in many battles during the American Revolutionary War on behalf of the British. Brant was also the person who helped the Six Nations secure the land grant surrounding the Grand River.

## GRANTING THE LAND

The land grant from the British to the Six Nations was made by Sir Frederick Haldimand. The land grant was for 675,000 acres, consisting of six miles of land on either side of the Grand River, for the entire length of the river. Some of those granted lands are now part of Waterloo Region.

Sir Frederick Haldimand (1718–1791) was the British Representative, or Chief, of what we now know as Ontario and Quebec. In 1784, he granted the Six Nations the land around the Grand River in the Haldimand Proclamation.

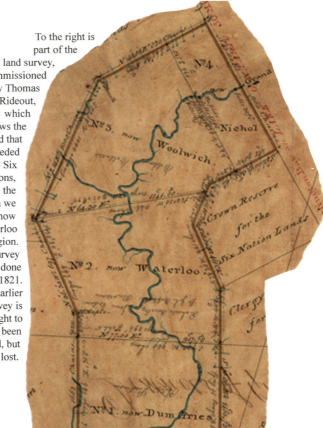

To the right is part of the land survey, commissioned by Thomas Rideout, which shows the land that was deeded to the Six Nations, around the area we now know as Waterloo Region. This survey was done in 1821. An earlier survey is thought to have been completed, but was later lost.

## SETTLING THE LAND

Joseph Brant led approximately 1,800 native people to the Grand River lands to build and settle small villages along the river. It appears that these Six Nation villages were south of where Waterloo Region is currently located.

This colour painting of a Six Nations village on the Grand River was done by Elizabeth Simcoe in 1793.

## SELLING THE LAND

Joseph Brant decided that some of the granted lands should be sold to provide money for the Six Nations. The money from the sale of the land was to be held in a trust fund by the government for the benefit of the Six Nations. To this day, the Six Nations believe that the government did not properly protect the money in their trust fund or fairly sell their land.

One person who bought the Six Nations' land was Richard Beasley, a business man and politician. Mr. Beasley bought the land with the help of two partners. It was Mr. Beasley who then sold his land to the Mennonites, who were the next group of people to settle in Waterloo Region.

# MENNONITES

The first significant group of non-Aboriginal settlers in Waterloo Region were Mennonites from Lancaster, Pennsylvania, USA. Mennonite is a term that describes followers of a specific religion. Mennonites are known for their peaceful ways; in fact, the Mennonite religion prohibits followers from participating in warfare. Mennonites came to live in Waterloo Region, starting in 1800, because of the affordable, high-quality land and fresh water. They also came to the Region because they believed they could live in the Region peacefully.

Map of Pennsylvania within North America

Pennsylvania

## THE TRIP

The trip from Pennsylvania to Waterloo Region was a precarious one. The trip was over 400 miles and could take up to seven weeks. The travellers used Conestoga wagons to transport their belongings to their new homes. The Conestoga wagon is a covered wagon which is pulled by horses or oxen. Often people would walk beside the wagon because the wagon, loaded with the family's possessions, would be too heavy for the horses to pull with the extra weight of people riding inside of it.

This is an example of a Conestoga wagon, which the Mennonites used to travel to Waterloo Region.

## CLEARING THE LAND

Upon arrival to Waterloo Region, if the Mennonite family had land waiting for them, they would begin clearing their land to establish their farm. Clearing the land was a huge undertaking. Removing tree stumps was a real challenge and each tree stump could take several days to remove. If the land was a swamp, it also needed to be drained.

To the left is an illustration of what it may have looked like while the Mennonites tried to clear their land for farming.

## WORKING

Most Mennonites who originally came to the Region were farmers. Working the fields was very labour intensive. Most farmers usually also had a vegetable garden to help feed their family.

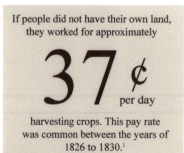

If people did not have their own land, they worked for approximately

# 37¢

per day

harvesting crops. This pay rate was common between the years of 1826 to 1830.[1]

Horses and oxen helped reduce the amount of manual labour needed when farming. Some Old Order Mennonites still use horses for farming.

## HOMES

During the warmer weather, Mennonites would often live in their Conestoga wagon or use the wagon as part of makeshift living quarters. However, for the harsh winters, Mennonites built stronger houses and their own furniture.

This handmade wooden crib is typical of Mennonite furniture. Many Mennonites made their own furniture when they first settled in the Region.

This home was built by Mennonite pioneer Christian Schneider. Although the photo was taken 1910, the home was built many years earlier.

# CULTURE

Mennonite culture emphasizes peace, service and simplicity. Mennonites are known for being hard workers. Mennonites maintain a simple lifestyle, and try not to attract attention to themselves. On Sundays, Mennonites gather at purposefully plain meetinghouses. Mennonites in the Region are known for making beautiful quilts, and early settlers often made a lovely form of folk art called Fraktur. A sub-group of Mennonites, known as Old Order Mennonites, do not use many, or any, of our modern technologies.

Mennonite meetinghouses are purposefully plain and simple, in keeping with Mennonite beliefs. Above, you can see a Mennonite meetinghouse and cemetery.

Fraktur is a form of folk art that was popular with Mennonite settlers. The artwork was often used to celebrate an important event such as a baptism. The Fraktur seen here was done by Abraham Latschaw in 1822.

Quilting is sewing pieces of material into a decorative and functional blanket. It is also a Mennonite tradition.

# PRESERVATION

There are many ways that the Region's Mennonite history is preserved including:

- Having local museums such as the Joseph Schneider Haus (see page 18), Brubacher House and The Mennonite Story;
- Housing the Mennonite Archives of Ontario at the University of Waterloo, Conrad Grebel University College; and
- Supporting the Waterloo Region Museum which has many Mennonite artifacts collected and displayed.

The Mennonite Story museum shares the history of the Mennonite faith and how many Mennonites emigrated from Europe to North America, and eventually came to Waterloo Region.

The Pioneer Settlers Memorial Tower was built as a memorial to the first pioneers in Waterloo Region. It was completed in 1926.

# SCOTLAND, ENGLAND & IRELAND

Many people from the countries of Scotland, England and Ireland immigrated to Waterloo Region. There were many different reasons that people from these countries decided to come to Waterloo Region including finding new opportunities and escaping poverty.

Map of Scotland, England and Ireland in Europe

Scotland, England and Ireland

## SCOTTISH SETTLERS

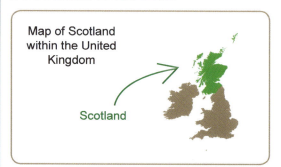

Map of Scotland within the United Kingdom

Scotland

Scottish settlers were encouraged to come to Waterloo Region by fellow Scotsman William Dickson. Mr. Dickson had left Scotland and created a successful business and legal career in the Niagara Region. Mr. Dickson bought approximately 94,000 acres in the Waterloo Region area in 1816. He then advertised in his homeland, Scotland, that land and opportunity was available in Waterloo Region.

William Dickson (1769–1846) was a successful lawyer and merchant. Mr. Dickson offered financial assistance and farming tools to encourage immigration to the Region.

Bagpipes and kilts are part of traditional Scottish culture.

The trip from Scotland to Waterloo Region included a boat ride across the ocean in a sailing ship. The trip took many weeks. When steam ships became more common the trip length was shortened.

Living History

This home was built in 1858, in the Cambridge area of Waterloo Region. It was first home to the Scottish family, the McDougalls; and then later home to the Scottish family, the Bairds.

The building is now a museum called McDougall Cottage. Visitors can come and enjoy the granite and limestone cottage and its lovely gardens. There are special events regularly held at McDougall Cottage that celebrate the area's Scottish history.

Peter Jaffray (1800–1864) came to Waterloo Region from Scotland. He started several newspapers including the *Galt Reporter*, *Agricultural Advertiser*, and *Dumfries Mercantile*.[1]

# ENGLISH SETTLERS

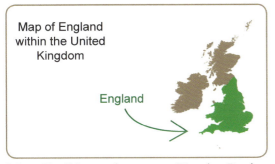

Map of England within the United Kingdom

England

Many English people came to Waterloo Region to find new opportunities. There were also emigration initiatives in England that encouraged poor people to leave England; this was done by paying for their trip to a new life in Canada. Sending poor people to Canada was considered a solution to poverty which had escalated in England due to industrialization.

Sergeant Frederick Hobson (1873–1917) was born in England and settled in Waterloo Region in 1904. He enlisted in the army for WWI and died in combat. He was awarded the Victoria Cross after his death.[1]

Orphans from England and the rest of Britain were sent to Canada starting in 1869. The Town of Galt, now part of the City of Cambridge, had a distribution home which would then send the children to live with local families. This practice was halted in Canada in the 1930s.

A statue of Queen Victoria (1819–1901), celebrating the Region's English and British heritage, can be found in Victoria Park, in the City of Kitchener. The statue was erected in 1911.

# IRISH SETTLERS

Map of Ireland within the United Kingdom

Ireland

This map reflects Ireland prior to 1922, After 1922, Ireland separated into Ireland and Northern Ireland.

There was significant emigration from Ireland to Canada during the Great Irish Potato Famine which was from 1846 to 1852. The famine occurred because the potato crops, which the Irish relied on heavily for food, failed. It has been estimated that over two million people left Ireland because of the famine. While many Irish people went to England and the United States, some Irish people settled in Canada, and in particular, Waterloo Region.

Thomas Hillard (1841–1936 ) was born in Ireland and came to Canada in 1847. He became a teacher, Waterloo School Inspector, founder of Dominion Life (an insurance company) and publisher of the *Waterloo Chronical.*[2]

St. Patrick's Day is an Irish holiday that is celebrated in the Region. It is often associated with shamrocks and leprechauns. The day was originally meant to celebrate St. Patrick, a Christian priest who lived in the 400s.

Here is a picture of a family saying good bye to Irish emigrants. The engraving was made by Henry Doyle around 1868.

# GERMANY

Many people from Germany came to Waterloo Region starting in the 1830s with the hope of creating a better life for themselves and their families. German settlers had a huge business and cultural impact on the Region. At one point, Waterloo Region was referred to as the German Capital of Canada.

Map of Germany within Europe

Germany

## SETTLING IN AND BUILDING BUSINESSES

German families often found their immigration to Waterloo Region eased by the fact that many residents of the Region, in particular Mennonite settlers and fellow German immigrants, already spoke German. Also, many of the German immigrants were highly skilled in a trade such as furniture building, which was valued in Waterloo Region.

Jacob Hailer (1804–1882) is believed to be the first settler who came directly from Germany to Waterloo Region (in 1830). He established and ran a successful furniture company.

Emil Vogelsang (1834–1894) was a button maker who came from Germany to the Region in 1866. He created and ran several successful button making businesses.[1]

Reinhold Lang (1817–1883) came to Waterloo Region from Germany. In 1849, he established a Tannery with his son. At one point the Lang Tannery was the biggest sole leather producer, not only in Canada, but also in the British Empire.[2] To the left, you can see work being completed at the Tannery. The Tannery closed in 1954. Interestingly, the Tannery buildings are now home to several high-tech companies including Google and Desire2Learn.

# CULTURE

German culture has been celebrated and preserved in Waterloo Region over the years. There are several German restaurants, clubs and special events in Waterloo Region.

The Concordia Club was founded in 1873 to celebrate and preserve German language, customs and traditions in the Region. The Club has been up and running continuously from 1873 to the present, with the exception of the two World Wars.[1]

The Christkindl Market is held each year in December, in the City of Kitchener. The market has gifts, crafts, food and toys for sale. Christmas markets are a common German tradition.

In 1911, approximately

# 70%

of people living in the villages of Berlin (later Kitchener) and Waterloo had a German background.[2]

German settlers celebrated their heritage in Waterloo Region. However, with the onset of World War I this did change a bit. In 1916, the Region's Town of Berlin, named after the German City of Berlin, changed its name to Kitchener.

## AND THEN THERE'S OKTOBERFEST

The Kitchener-Waterloo Oktoberfest Festival is a traditional German festival that is celebrated in Waterloo Region. It is the largest Oktoberfest festival outside of Germany. Activities held during the festival include an Oktoberfest Parade and several family-friendly events. At night, there are many "Festhallen" across the Region that have traditional German food, beer, music and lots of fun.

This woman is wearing a drindl which is a traditional German dress that is often worn during Oktoberfest.

Schnitzel is a classic German food that is served during Oktoberfest.

Onkel Hans is the mascot for the Kitchener-Waterloo Oktoberfest Festival. He is a common sight at the Oktoberfest Parade and during the many activities that occur during Oktoberfest.

Beer is a common sight in Oktoberfest Festhallen.

" *Gemuetlichkeit* "

Gemuetlichkeit is the theme of Oktoberfest. It is a German word that means a combination of coziness, belonging and cheerfulness.

# EARLY SETTLERS
# MANY MORE

Settlers came to Waterloo Region from all over Canada and the world. Below are some more examples of where settlers lived prior to immigrating to the Region.

Map of Newfoundland within Canada

Newfoundland

## NEWFOUNDLAND

Many Waterloo Region settlers came from Newfoundland. During World War II, many young women were recruited from Newfoundland to work in Waterloo Region's textile mills. In 1966, the mining operations on Bell Island, Newfoundland, closed. This resulted in another wave of Newfoundlanders moving to the Region looking for new opportunities.

It is estimated that in the 1970s up to

# 15,000

of the City of Cambridge's residents came from Newfoundland.[1]

This is a photo of a woman working at Dominion Woollens and Worstens, the Region's largest textile mill during World War II. Many women from Newfoundland came to Waterloo Region to work for textile companies.

Many people from Bell Island, Newfoundland, seen to the left, came to live in Waterloo Region after the mining operations on Bell Island closed in 1966.

## WAR SPOUSES

Many people from Waterloo Region participated in the war effort during World War I and II. Some of these men and women were stationed overseas. If they married when they were overseas, the soldiers would often bring their spouses home to Waterloo Region after the war ended.

A Canadian military man with his wife.

## FREEDOM SEEKERS

Former black slaves from the United States came to Canada, including parts of Waterloo Region, so that they could be free. Some settled in the area of the Queen's Bush which later became Wellesley Township. In this area, the residents cleared and farmed land that belonged to the government. Unfortunately, when the government made the land available for sale, many of these pioneers could not afford the land; because of this situation many had left the Region by 1865.

# PORTUGAL

Significant Portuguese immigration to Waterloo Region began in the 1950s. The Portuguese immigrants were mostly from the Azores part of Portugal; and they usually settled in the City of Cambridge.

One person who played an important role in bringing Portuguese immigrants to Waterloo Region is Manual Cabral. Mr. Cabral helped many people from Portugal to settle in the Region and find employment.

Map of Portugal within Europe

Portugal

Manual Cabral (1894–1979) was born in America to parents who had immigrated from Portugal. Mr. Cabral came to the Region in 1928. He used his proficiency in both English and Portuguese to help many Portuguese immigrants settle in the Region.

This monument was erected in 1979 in the City of Cambridge. It is meant to celebrate the Portuguese community in the City of Cambridge.

XXV ANNIVERSARY OF THE PORTUGUESE COMMUNITY CAMBRIDGE (GALT) 1954 1979 IN APPRECIATION FOR THE COURAGE OF THE PIONEERS AND GRATITUDE TO CANADA AND THEIR PEOPLE JULY 6 TH 1979

The Portuguese Club of Cambridge holds events for the Portuguese community in the Region. To the left is Portugal's flag.

Portugal Day is a traditional Portuguese holiday celebrating Luís Vaz de Camões and his famous poems. Portugal Day is celebrated in the City of Cambridge with a parade and other events. This portrait of Luís Vaz de Camões is by Fernão Gomes.

# MANY MORE

Settlers came to Waterloo Region from around the world looking for new opportunities. The diversity found in the Region further enhances the services and quality of life for new immigrants who decide to settle in the Region.

| More countries from which immigrants to the Region are originally from | | |
|---|---|---|
| • Italy | • Romania | • China |
| • Korea | • Japan | • Poland |
| • Serbia | • Russia | • India |
| • Ghana | • Vietnam | • Greece |
| • Jamaica | • Czech Republic | • El Salvador |

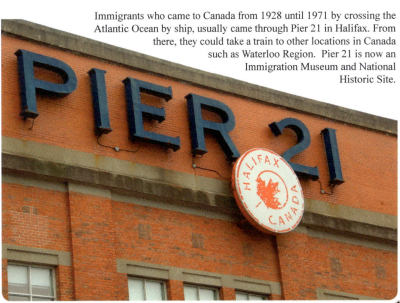

Immigrants who came to Canada from 1928 until 1971 by crossing the Atlantic Ocean by ship, usually came through Pier 21 in Halifax. From there, they could take a train to other locations in Canada such as Waterloo Region. Pier 21 is now an Immigration Museum and National Historic Site.

# EVERYDAY LIFE
# PEOPLE & FAMILIES

Waterloo Region is a success because of its people. People of all ages, talents and backgrounds are part of the Waterloo Region community; and they live in different kinds of families and households.

## DIVERSE BACKGROUNDS

Most of the over five hundred thousand people who currently live in Waterloo Region were born in Canada. However, Waterloo Region is still a magnet for immigrants because of the wonderful educational and employment opportunities available. In fact, over one hundred thousand of the Region's current residents were not born in Canada.[1] The top three places of birth of current immigrants are the United Kingdom, Portugal and India.[2]

There are many different kinds of families in Waterloo Region

In the Region, more than

# 6,695

people identify themselves as Aboriginal.[3]

Norman Lynn (1928–1999) was a dedicated community builder and the founding chairman of the Kitchener-Waterloo Multicultural Centre. Mr. Lynn also helped establish the Central Ontario Chinese Cultural Centre.

The Region celebrates local multiculturalism with the annual Kitchener-Waterloo Multicultural Festival. The festival is held in Victoria Park which is in the City of Kitchener. At the festival, people can sample food from a broad range of cultures.

## ALL AGES

People of all ages live in Waterloo Region. The median age of Waterloo Region residents is slightly younger than the Canadian or Ontario median age.[4]

The median age is

# 37.7

years old in Waterloo Region.[5]

People of all ages live in Waterloo Region.

| Age Group | Percentage of People[6] |
|-----------|-------------------------|
| 0-9 years | 12% |
| 10-19 years | 13% |
| 20-29 years | 14% |
| 30-39 years | 15% |
| 40-49 years | 15% |
| 50-59 years | 14% |
| 60-69 years | 9% |
| 70-79 years | 5% |
| 80+ years | 3% |

# LIVING ARRANGEMENTS

Residents of Waterloo Region have many different living arrangements. Some people in the Region live alone, while others live with family or friends, and other people live in institutions such as student residences.

The average number of people living together is

# 2.6

per household.[1]

The most common number of people living together in the Region two.[2]

| Number of People Living Together | Number of Households[3] |
|---|---|
| Alone | 45,285 |
| Two people living together | 63,160 |
| Three people living together | 32,565 |
| Four people living together | 32,475 |
| Five people living together | 12,050 |
| Six or more people living together | 6,060 |

# FAMILIES

There are many different kinds of families in Waterloo Region including married couples with or without children, common-law couples with or without children, and lone-parent families. There are also multi-generational households and other family arrangements.

*It's a First* #1

The Independent Living Centre of Waterloo Region was the first Independent Living Centre in Canada. It was started with the help of the Mennonite Central Committee. The Centre helps people with disabilities to live more independently by providing a broad range of services including assisted-living facilities, as well as outreach services offered in clients' homes.

There are approximately 21,755 lone-parent families in the Region.[4]

There are over 103,945 married couple familes in Waterloo Region.[5]

There are about 16,515 common-law couples in the Region.[6]

*Piece of History*

What an extended family! Below is just part of a photograph of a 1930 Shantz family reunion held in Waterloo Park. Christian Shantz was the first Shantz pioneer in Waterloo Region. He came to the Region in 1806. Christian Shantz and his wife, Magdalena, had twelve children.

# EVERYDAY LIFE
# HOMES

Waterloo Region is filled with many wonderful homes. In fact, there are different housing options to meet a broad range of individual and family needs.

There are many beautiful homes in Waterloo Region.

## TYPES OF HOMES

By far the most common type of home in Waterloo Region is a single-detached home. However, there are also many semi-detached homes, row homes, condominiums and apartments. There are also specialized homes such as student and retirement residences.

Row homes are increasing in popularity across the Region.

Condominium and apartment buildings are currently located, and are being built, close to each of the three cities' downtown areas to give residents the option of a very walkable lifestyle. This condominium is located in downtown Kitchener.

| Type of Home | Number of Residences[1] |
|---|---|
| Single-detached home | 109,400 |
| Semi-detached home | 12,910 |
| Row home | 20,240 |
| Apartment in a building with less than five stories | 24,640 |
| Apartment in a building with five or more stories | 18,540 |
| Moveable homes | 350 |

There are many charming older homes in the Region like these found in the City of Cambridge.

There are several senior and student residences in Region.

## Living History

The home of Joseph Schneider is one of the oldest homes in the Region that is still standing. It was built around 1820 by Joseph Schneider. Mr. Schneider came to Waterloo Region in 1807 and was one of the Region's first pioneers; he was also a farmer and a sawmill owner. In 1981, Mr. Schneider's home was turned into a living history museum, called Joseph Schneider Haus Museum and Gallery. It has costumed interpreters who demonstrate how people may have lived in the home in the 1900s.

Joseph Schneider Haus Museum is located in downtown Kitchener by Victoria Park. The combination of the museum and the park make for a lovely visit.

## BUYING HOMES

Many people in Waterloo Region make the decision to purchase a home. In fact, seventy-one percent of Regional residents live in homes that are owner occupied.[1] The average price for a single-detached home is $352,807, and the average price for a condominium is $214,226.[2]

There are many relators who are skilled at helping people in the Region buy and sell homes.

*Homes Plus is just one of the many resources that Waterloo Region home buyers have available.*

## " Top Investment Town "

The cities of Kitchener, Cambridge and Waterloo were all listed as top Ontario real estate investment towns according to The Real Estate Investment Network.[4]

## RENTING HOMES

There is a robust rental market in Waterloo Region. There are many quality homes, apartments, and condominiums for rent in the Region. In fact, there are approximately 28,185 private rental units in the Region.[5] The average monthly rental price for different types of rental homes are listed in the table below.

The Bauer Lofts is the name of the modern condominium complex to the right. It is located in the City of Waterloo.

| Type of Rental Home | Average Monthly Cost[6] |
| --- | --- |
| Bachelor | $644.00 |
| One Bedroom | $773.00 |
| Two Bedroom | $908.00 |
| Three Bedroom | $1,053.00 |

# 29%
of people live in homes that are rented.[7]

## AFFORDABLE HOUSING

The Region of Waterloo Municipal Government works to create affordable rental options for low income individuals and families. There is also Heartwood Place which is a privately established not-for-profit organization in the Region. Heartwood Place builds and administers community housing for people in need of a safe, secure home when they do not have enough income to secure housing independently.

Habitat for Humanity has built many homes in the Region for families. In their program, future owners help build their own home, instead for making a down payment. The Canadian headquarters for Habitat for Humanity is in Waterloo Region.

# TRANSPORTATION

There are many different ways to get around Waterloo Region including: walking, biking, and driving a car. There is also public transportation available, which includes buses and a future light rail transit system.

## PEOPLE POWERED

Waterloo Region is very walkable with sidewalks on most neighborhoods streets. There are also several downtown areas in the Region where stores, businesses and residences are located close together; these areas are particularly suited to walking.

Many people bicycle in Waterloo Region. Regional experts estimate that if a trip is less than five kilometers, it is possible that biking can be as quick as driving.[2] Moreover, there are many roads in the Region which have separate, designated bike lanes. Unfortunately, during the winter, it can be difficult to bicycle because the ice and snow can make the roads slippery.

## PUBLIC TRANSPORTATION

Grand River Transit (GRT) is Waterloo Region's public transportation system. The GRT buses run across the cities of Kitchener, Waterloo and Cambridge.

Each year, GRT buses travel approximately twelve million kilometers.[3] The buses are equipped to carry bicycles for people who would like to bike to their bus stop.

GRT has also invested in hybrid buses. Hybrid buses help minimize the amount of fuel used by the GRT buses and the amount of pollution emitted by GRT vehicles.

There are over 500 kilometers of bike trails and bike pathways in the Region.[1]

Many children ride school buses to and from school. Busing is free for children who live a specified distance from school and attend a school run by a publicly funded school board.

A Grand River Transit hybrid bus.

Piece of History

Between the years of 1889 and 1895, horse-drawn railway cars were operated in the Region. This is a photograph of a railway car on King St. in Waterloo. After 1895, electric cars replaced the horse-drawn cars.[4]

## CARS, CARS, CARS

Cars are the dominant mode of transportation in Waterloo Region, and most places are easily accessible by car. For people who do not have their own car, there is Community CarShare, which provides the opportunity for its members to access their fleet of cars.

There are many city streets and regional roads in Waterloo Region. The Region also has Highway 85/86, which turns into Highway 7/8 in the west part of the Region. This highway provides a fast way to drive through the Region. Another highway, Highway 401, goes through the City of Cambridge and the City of Kitchener, as well as the Township of North Dumfries. Driving east on Highway 401 is an easy way to get the City of Toronto.

Highway 85/86, which turns into Highway 7/8 in the west part of the Region, provides a fast way for drivers to get around Waterloo Region.

## TRAVELLING OUT OF TOWN

There are a lot of ways to get out of the Region. You can, of course, drive. But you can also take the train. Via Rail goes through the City of Kitchener and across Canada. GO Transit also has train service going from Kitchener to Toronto.

There are private intercity bus services such as Greyhound; as well as publicly funded intercity buses run by GO Transit. If you prefer to fly, there are flights from the Region of Waterloo International Airport to destinations in Canada and the USA. Also, the Toronto Pearson International Airport is only an hour from Waterloo Region by car.

*Piece of History*

This train is on display at the Waterloo Region Museum. It is an example of the kind of train that ran through the Region a hundred years ago.

The introduction of the railway to the Region had a big impact on increasing business and trade for Waterloo Region companies. The train ran through the Town of Berlin, later called the City of Kitchener.

Flying from the Region of Waterloo International Airport is a convenient way to travel.

You can take modern VIA Rail trains from the Region right across Canada.

*Living History*

You can still see horse-drawn buggies on township roads in Waterloo Region. This is because many Old Order Mennonites do not wish to use modern transportation options, so they continue to use the transportation methods of previous generations.

## FUTURE TRANSPORTATION

In Waterloo Region, new transportation vehicles and systems are being developed and built. There are many companies that build vehicles in the Region including Toyota, and Ontario Drive and Gear (for more information see page 35). Also, research at the University of Waterloo is helping develop new transportation options, such as the Midnight Sun which runs on the sun's energy.

The Region of Waterloo Municipal Government is building a new light rail transit system to serve the most populated parts of the Region. The light rail transit system is expected to be completed in 2017.

The Midnight Sun is a solar car that has been developed in Waterloo Region by University of Waterloo students.

# EVERYDAY LIFE
# SHOPPING

There are many wonderful places to buy the things you want and need in Waterloo Region. Some of the great places you can go shopping include: charming downtowns, farmers' markets, modern malls, outlet stores and large discount chains. Online shopping is also popular in the Region.

There are many farmers' markets in the Region including the St Jacobs Farmers' Market, Cambridge Farmers' Market, Herrle's Country Farm Market, and the Kitchener Market.

## SHOPPING MALLS

There are large shopping malls located in each of the three cities in Waterloo Region. The malls usually have a mix of department stores, clothing stores, and speciality stores. Some malls in the Region also have other features such as movies theaters and food courts; the Cambridge Centre Mall even has an ice rink.

There are many high-fashion clothing and accessory stores in local malls.

## CHARMING DOWNTOWNS

There are many charming downtown shopping areas in Waterloo Region. Local stores, parks, offices, and other amenities make these downtowns wonderful places to shop and spend time.

The downtown area of New Hamburg has many charming shops. In fact, a section of downtown New Hamburg is a Heritage Conservation District.

## DISCOUNT STORES

There are many discount stores in Waterloo Region where you can find great deals including: big box and bulk stores, dollar stores, as well as popular discount retailers such as Walmart and Target.

Good deals can be found in Waterloo Region.

## ONLINE

If you prefer to do your shopping online, Waterloo Region has high-speed internet readily available, as well as many excellent delivery options including Canada Post, FedEx, Purolator and more.

Online shopping is easy in Waterloo Region.

*Piece of History*

Home Hardware was founded in Waterloo Region. The company was formed in 1964 when over a hundred independent hardware store owners, lead by Walter Hachborn, came together to buy Hollinger Hardware of St. Jacobs, which is in the Township of Woolwich. The idea was to pool the purchasing power and brand recognition of the many independent hardware stores into the Home Hardware brand.

There are now over 1,000 Home Hardware store locations that can be found across Canada. The stores can be easily identified by their bright red, white and yellow signs.

# PETS

Waterloo Region is a pet-friendly place. Many people in the Region have pets such as dogs, cats, birds, rabbits, and fish. There are many support services to help keep your pet healthy and happy; as well as specialized training opportunities for service animals. However, not all animals are allowed to be pets in the Region.

Goldfish and other aquatic life are popular pets in Waterloo Region.

## Dogs

Many people in Waterloo Region have dogs as pets. Each city and township within the Region has bylaws regarding having pet dogs. Generally speaking, every dog owner is required to buy a licence for each dog they own, keep their dog on a leash in public places, and pick up any excrement their dogs may leave behind.

There are many wonderful resources for dog owners including leash free parks, dog hospitals and doggie daycare.

Puppies are popular in Waterloo Region. Puppies need to have a dog license when they reach 12 weeks of age.

### NATIONAL SERVICE DOGS

National Service Dogs is a charity located in Waterloo Region that nurtures and trains service dogs to assist individuals with autism, or veterans with post-tramatic stress syndrome.

The organization has successfully placed over 300 service dogs.[1] They have their own puppy program that helps support their training program. The organization has many volunteers.

To the left is Brodie, with his National Service Dog Shadow.

## Cats

Cats and kittens are popular pets in Waterloo Region. Similar to dogs, each city and township has their own bylaws regarding cats. Generally, cats do not need to have a licence; however, some parts of the Region have a limit as to the number of cats that can live in one home. There are many resources for cat owners in the Region including specialized cat clinics, general veterinary services, and many stores that sell items to improve cat health.

There are many cats in the Region. Generally, cats do not need to be licensed.

## Other Pets

There are many other pets that people in Waterloo Region welcome into their homes such as rabbits, turtles and hamsters. Not all animals are allowed to be pets in the Region, although which pets are prohibited varies by each city and township. Generally speaking, prohibited pets include venomous animals, extra long snakes, and non-indigenous animals such as crocodiles.

Rabbits can be pets in Waterloo Region.

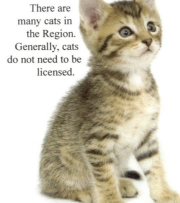

## Local Humane Societies

There are two local humane societies in the Region: the Kitchener-Waterloo Humane Society and the Cambridge and District Humane Society. These organizations provide a place for homeless cats, dogs and other animals. The humane societies have successful adoption programs that help dogs and cats find new homes; as well as education programs for local residents on the best ways to treat and train their pets.

In 1831, Waterloo Council declared that dog owners needed to pay a tax of

# $1 for the first male dog

and $2 for the first female dog.[2]

# WEATHER

Waterloo Region's weather is humid continental, which means that Waterloo Region has large seasonal differences with a hot summer and a cold winter. This wide range of weather can bring a lot of variety to the activities residents engage in during the year.

The deciduous trees in Waterloo Region grow green leaves in the spring.

## SPRING

Spring in the Region is from March 20th to June 20th. New leaves on trees, and budding flowers, characterize spring in Waterloo Region. There are usually moderate temperatures during spring, as noted in the table below.

Crocuses poke out of the ground in the spring.

Tulips bloom in the spring in Waterloo Region.

| Month | Average Daily High | Average Daily Low[1] |
|-------|--------------------|----------------------|
| April | 11.1 °C | 0.4 °C |
| May | 18.6 °C | 6.3 °C |
| June | 23.4 °C | 11.2 °C |

*Piece of History*

Waterloo Region experienced a huge flood in the City of Cambridge, in the Galt area, on May 17, 1974. Many streets were four feet under water and many homes and businesses were damaged.

Images from this flood, such as the one to the right, circulated across Canada.

After this 1974 flood, many changes were made by the City of Cambridge, Regional Government and the Grand River Conservation Authority to prevent such dramatic flooding, and the related damage, in the future.

## SUMMER

Summer in Waterloo Region is from June 21st to September 21st. It can get quite hot. Summer is the perfect season for outdoor activities such as swimming and boating. It can occasionally get quite humid.

| Month | Average Daily High | Average Daily Low[2] |
|-------|--------------------|----------------------|
| July | 25.9 °C | 13.7 °C |
| August | 24.7 °C | 12.7 °C |
| September | 20.2 °C | 8.4 °C |

Swimming and other water activities are very popular in the summer.

Highest temperature in the Region without humidex[3]

**36.5 °C**

Highest temperature in the Region with humidex[4]

**48.3 °C**

# FALL

Fall in Waterloo Region is from September 22nd to December 20th. Fall is a wonderful time for taking walks because the leaves on deciduous trees turn from green to orange, yellow and red. The result is lovely, colourful forests and parks. Fall temperatures are cooler than in the summer, as noted in the table below.

| Month | Average Daily High | Average Daily Low [1] |
|---|---|---|
| October | 13.4 °C | 2.9 °C |
| November | 6.1 °C | 1.5 °C |
| December | -0.2 °C | -7.3 °C |

Most daily rainfall in the Region [2]

**89.8 mm**

Strongest wind gusts in the Region [3]

**120 km/h**

Waterloo Park in the fall is full of colour as the deciduous trees leaves turn from green to orange, yellow and red.

# WINTER

Winter in Waterloo Region is from December 21st to March 19th. There is often quite a bit of snow and ice in the winter. Winter is the perfect season for skating and skiing outdoors. Winter temperatures in Waterloo Region are quite cold, as noted in the table below.

| Month | Average Daily High | Average Daily Low [4] |
|---|---|---|
| January | - 3.1 °C | - 11.0 °C |
| February | - 2.0 °C | - 10.7 °C |
| March | 3.3 °C | - 5.8 °C |

Lowest temperature in the Region without windchill [5]

**-31.9 °C**

Lowest temperature in the Region with windchill [6]

**-40.5 °C**

Victoria Park in the winter is lovely when covered with snow and ice. During the winter holidays, it is lit up with beautiful lights in the evening.

## Piece of History

To the left, you can see a man using a horse-drawn sled. This picture was taken in 1910 on King St. in Waterloo.

The CPR Holiday Train is one of the many interesting light displays you can see in the winter in the Region.

# INFORMATION & COMMUNICATION

There are a wide variety of ways to stay informed in Waterloo Region including: accessing the internet, reading local newspapers, watching television or listening to the radio. There is great cellphone coverage for people who use smartphones, and mail service for people who prefer to send letters.

## INTERNET

Waterloo Region is an very wired community. There is an extensive network of fibre optic cables on which internet services can be accessed. The Region has many WiFi hotspots in restaurants, coffee shops and other public spaces. The Region also has great cellphone coverage for people who prefer to access the internet using their phone.

## LIBRARIES

The library systems in Waterloo Region are fantastic. Each city has its own library system with several branches, and the townships share a library system which has many branches as well. In most cases, obtaining a library card is free, and so is borrowing materials and using the computers.

One of the first libraries in the Region was the Galt Subscription and Circulating Library founded in

# 1836

There were about a 150 members.[1]

Here is the Hespeler Branch of the Cambridge Public Library. The traditional Hespeler Library was built in 1923 with help of a Carnegie Foundation grant. In 2007, the library was expanded and a modern glass exterior was added to the building.

## REGULAR MAIL AND PACKAGES

Regular mail delivery is provided by Canada Post. Package delivery is done by several organizations in Waterloo Region including Canada Post, FedEx, UPS and Purolator.

To the left is a Canada Post delivery person with a Canada Post truck. Canada Post's delivery service covers all of Waterloo Region.

### Living History

This historic building, and former post office, was designed by Thomas Fuller. Mr. Fuller also designed some of the Parliament buildings in Ottawa. This building is being renovated into a public library with a restaurant. It is in the Galt area of the City of Cambridge.

## NEWSPAPERS AND PRINT MEDIA

There are many excellent newspapers in Waterloo Region. The *Waterloo Region Record* is the Region's largest newspaper and it also has an online presence. Below is a list of many of the great papers in Waterloo Region.

| Local Newspaper | Coverage Area |
| --- | --- |
| *Waterloo Region Record* | Waterloo Region |
| *Kitchener Citizen* | City of Kitchener |
| *Waterloo Chronicle* | City of Waterloo |
| *Elmira Independent* | Town of Elmira and area |
| *New Hamburg Independent* | Wilmot Township |
| *Cambridge Citizen* | City of Cambridge |
| *Cambridge Times* | City of Cambridge |
| *Kitchener Post* | City of Kitchener |
| *Ayr News* | Town of Ayr and area |
| *Observer* | Wellesley and Woolwich Townships |
| *SNAP Kitchener Waterloo* | Waterloo Region |
| *Baden Outlook* | Town of Baden and area |
| *The Cord Community* | Waterloo Region |
| And school-based newspapers | Across the Region |

## TELEVISION

Waterloo Region has two local TV stations. CTV Southwestern Ontario is a local TV Station which is based in Kitchener but covers the whole Region with its three local newscasts.

The second TV station is Rogers TV Waterloo Region. It is located in Kitchener and creates custom programming for the Region's residents including local shows such as *Daytime* and *Talk Local Waterloo Region*.

## TELEPHONES AND SMARTPHONES

Waterloo Region has extensive landline and cellphone coverage. Moreover, one of the world's first smartphones, the BlackBerry®, was developed in Waterloo Region (see page 39). The Blackberry is well known for its quality and security features.

*Piece of History*

A municipal phone system was available in Waterloo Region from 1914. However, historians note that rural schools were not connected to the telephone system until 1957.[1]

The *New Hamburg Independent* is an example of a successful local newspaper in Waterloo Region.

## RADIO

Waterloo Region has many local radio stations which provide a broad range of programming including: news and talk, a variety of music formats, and faith-based programming. Below is a list of some of the radio stations in the Region.

| Local Radio Stations | Format |
| --- | --- |
| 570 News AM (CKGL AM) | Local news and talk shows |
| 105.3 KOOL FM (CFCA FM) | Adult contemporary music |
| 96.7 FM (CHYM FM) | Variety of music and talk |
| 99.5 KFUN (KFUN FM) | Music from the 60s and 70s |
| 106.7 FM (COUNTRY FM) | Country music |
| 94.3 Faith FM (CJTW FM) | Faith-based broadcasting |
| 91.5 The Beat FM (CKBT FM) | Current music |
| 89.1 FM (CBC Radio) | News and talk |
| and more stations | Such as school radio stations |

**" Intelligent Community of the Year "**

The City of Waterloo won the coveted title of Intelligent Community of the Year from the Intelligent Communities Forum in 2007. The award was for a community that maximized its broadband internet connectivity and information technology resources.[2]

# KINDERGARTEN TO GRADE TWELVE

Waterloo Region has great educational opportunities for children and teens. There are several publicly funded education providers in the Region including: the Waterloo Region District School Board and the Waterloo Catholic District School Board. There are also several private schools that provide education for this age group.

Otto Klotz (1817–1892) played an important role in establishing public education in Waterloo Region. In 1884, he succeeded in creating the first free school in the Region. The school was in Preston, which is now a part of the City of Cambridge.[1]

## WATERLOO REGION DISTRICT SCHOOL BOARD

The Waterloo Region District School Board (WRDSB) provides free education to approximately 60,000 students every year.[2] WRDSB runs 103 elementary schools and 16 high schools.[3] WRDSB has several special education programs that help support the individual learning needs of almost 14,000 of its students.[4] The WRDSB also offers a French Immersion program.

There are about 3,500 teachers that work for WRDSB.[5] In addition to teaching classes, many teachers are involved in supervising extracurricular activities. The WRDSB also has 2,000 dedicated support staff.[6]

Grandview Public School in Cambridge is a WRDSB school which provides education for children in kindergarten to grade six.

The school year in Waterloo Region stretches from the beginning of September to the end of June.

The Waterloo Region District School Board educates approximately

# 60,000

students each school year.[7]

There are many programs in Waterloo Region that help preschoolers get ready for school.

To the left are four of Bluevale Collegiate Institute's students and their teacher. Bluevale is a WRDSB high school.

### Piece of History

"Determine the interest on $394.50, if the interest rate is 8% for six and a half years."[8]

Not everyone got to go to high school in 1881. To attend high school, you needed to pass a difficult entrance exam. A sample question from the high school entrance exam is seen above.

# WATERLOO CATHOLIC DISTRICT SCHOOL BOARD

The Waterloo Catholic District School Board (WCDSB) provides free eduction which includes a Catholic education component. WCDSB educates over 40,000 students, which is about twenty-seven percent of Waterloo Region students.[1] The WCDSB has many different special education programs that are tailored to help students. Approximately 3,500 staff members work for the WCDSB to meet students educational needs.[2]

*Over 2.5 million raised for charity since 1998.*

— WCDSB [3]

Here is an enthusiastic primary class, one of many primary classes offered by the WCDSB.

## Piece of History

This historic building is the City of Waterloo's first school house which was built in 1820. The school house is now on display in Waterloo Park. There were schools built outside the City of Waterloo, but within the Region, before this building.

St. Margaret of Scotland Catholic Elementary School in the City of Cambridge provides education for children in kindergarten to grade eight. It is a WCDSB school.

The Waterloo Region Catholic District School Board educates approximately

# 40,000

students each school year.[4]

# PRIVATE SCHOOLS

There is a broad selection of private schools available in Waterloo Region. Many of the Region's private schools are listed below.

| Private Grade Schools | |
| --- | --- |
| • Fellowship Christian School | • St. John's-Kilmarnock School |
| • Foundation Christian School | • St. Jude's School |
| • K-W Montessori School | • Scholars' Hall |
| • Kitchener-Waterloo Bilingual School | • Stanford Academy |
| • Laurentian Hills Christian School | • Sunshine Montessori School |
| • Rockway Mennonite Collegiate | • Woodland Christian High School |

There are many places for students to learn French in Waterloo Region.

# LANGUAGE SCHOOLS

There are many schools that teach languages beyond English. There is French instruction in both WRDSB and WCDSB schools. Moreover, there are specialized schools such as:

- Kitchener-Waterloo Bilingual School (a privately funded French and English school);
- École Élémentaire Catholique Cardinal-Léger (Catholic French School Board); and
- École Élémentaire L'Harmonie (Public French School Board).

The Waterloo Region District School Board also offers an International Languages Program where a wide range of languages can be learned including: Mandarin, German, Greek and Spanish.

# COLLEGES & APPRENTICESHIPS

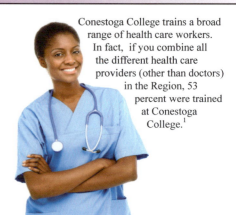

Conestoga College trains a broad range of health care workers. In fact, if you combine all the different health care providers (other than doctors) in the Region, 53 percent were trained at Conestoga College.[1]

There are several colleges in Waterloo Region. By far the largest college in the Region is the Conestoga College Institute of Technology and Advanced Learning. Conestoga College is a publicly funded college. There are also many private career colleges in the Region.

## CONESTOGA COLLEGE

Conestoga College is one of the best colleges in Ontario. It provides career training in many areas including: business, hospitality, engineering technology, health care and community services. While there are many full-time programs, there are also many opportunities to complete studies on a part-time basis. Conestoga College offers a variety of educational formats from co-operative education to providing courses online.

A Masters of Business Administration can be completed at the College in cooperation with University of Windsor.

Conestoga College's main campus is seen here. It is called the Doon Campus and it is located in the City of Kitchener. The College also has campuses in the cities of Cambridge, Guelph, Stratford, Waterloo and Ingersoll.

## Quick Facts about Conestoga College[2]

| | |
|---|---|
| 9,300 full-time students | 35,000 part-time students |
| 120 full-time diploma programs | 26 apprenticeship programs |
| 130 part-time programs | 23 graduate certificates |
| 84,000 alumni | 6 satellite campuses |

Conestoga College was founded in

# 1967

to provided career-related skills and diplomas.[3]

Conestoga College estimates that 87% of their students are employed six months after graduation.[4]

Conestoga College has general interest courses for community residents. The course offerings range from gardening to personal finance.

# PRIVATE COLLEGES

There are many different career colleges in the Region. Students have the opportunity to develop specialized skills in areas such as cooking, hospitality, personal care and information technology.

Liaison College has a satellite campus located in Waterloo Region that provides training for students in the culinary arts.[2]

Students can learn esthetic skills at Gina's College. Here is Cristina Ramirez, Director of the College, instructing students in an aesthetics course.[1]

Medix College is a career college located in Waterloo Region which offers training in several medical professions including dental assistant, massage therapy, personal support worker, and pharmacy assistant.[4]

Trios College has a campus in Waterloo Region. It has a broad range of technology programs in areas such as network support and video game design.[3]

# APPRENTICESHIPS

Apprenticeships provide on-the-job training. They are a great way to build skills to succeed in the workplace. There are many different ways to obtain an apprenticeship. For example, high school students can apply for an apprenticeship training program as part of their high school experience.

After high school, traditional apprenticeship training requires the future apprentice to find an employer who is willing to sponsor them and then register with the *Ontario Ministry of Training, Colleges and Universities Apprenticeship Office.*

There are also apprenticeships that can be combined with a diploma from a local college called Co-Op Diploma Apprenticeship Programs.

Co-op apprenticeship programs are offered at Conestoga College.

Plumbing is one of the many areas in which there are apprenticeships available in Waterloo Region.

# EDUCATION
# UNIVERSITIES

There are two universities in Waterloo Region, the University of Waterloo and Wilfrid Laurier University. Both are exceptional educational institutions that are well respected across Canada and beyond. The universities bring many people to Waterloo Region including: students from across the world, esteemed professors and researchers, and companies wishing to be close to the universities because of their skilled graduates.

## WILFRID LAURIER UNIVERSITY

Wilfrid Laurier University (WLU) was the first university established in the Region. WLU offers a broad range of programs in the areas of science, social work, arts and economics. It is particularly well known for its business and music programs. Also, the Waterloo Lutheran Seminary is affiliated with Wilfrid Laurier University.

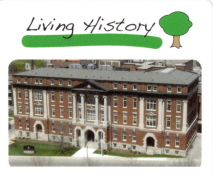

Living History

The WLU Faculty of Social Work is located in downtown Kitchener in a historic building which was initially built in 1907 to house St. Jerome's High School. In 2006, the Faculty of Social Work moved into this building.

WLU has an esteemed music program.

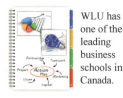

WLU has one of the leading business schools in Canada.

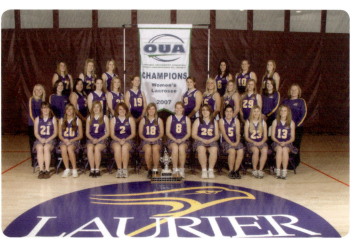

Wilfrid Laurier has many successful sports teams. This is a photo of the 2007 female WLU Ontario Champion Lacrosse team.

Wilfrid Laurier University has great facilities. Above is the building housing the Faculty of Music.

### Quick Facts about WLU[1]

- WLU has approximately 17,000 undergraduate and graduate students.

- It has campuses in Waterloo, Kitchener, Brantford, Toronto, and Chongqing, China.

- WLU provides the only Masters of Music Therapy in Canada.

- It created the first MBA in Canada with a 12 month time frame.

- WLU has six faculties: Arts, Music, Science, Education, Social Work, Graduate Studies and the School of Business and Economics.

WLU graduate Mike Morrice is the founder of Sustainable Waterloo Region, an organization that helps companies and institutions make environmentally-friendly decisions.

Piece of History

Above is a photograph of the official opening of the Evangelical Lutheran Seminary of Canada in 1911. The seminary, now known as Waterloo Lutheran Seminary, is still affiliated with WLU.

# UNIVERSITY OF WATERLOO

The University of Waterloo is Waterloo Region's largest university. It was founded in 1957 to train leaders in innovation and technology. The University of Waterloo has rounded out its offerings with programs in the arts, sciences and the environment; as well as professional programs in areas such as optometry, architecture and pharmacy.

The Student Life Centre at the University of Waterloo is an example of the exceptional facilities available to University of Waterloo students.

The average grade of a student entering the University of Waterloo is:[1]

# 87.2%

Media personality and businessman Kevin O'Leary (born 1954) is a graduate of University of Waterloo.

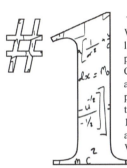

The University of Waterloo has the largest co-operative program in the world.[3] Co-operative education alternates study periods with work terms. There are about 17,300 co-op students at the University of Waterloo.[4]

> " The Faculty of Mathematics is the world's largest faculty in the mathematical, statistical, and computer sciences. "

— University of Waterloo [2]

Above is one of the University of Waterloo's Faculty of Engineering buildings. The University of Waterloo has the largest Engineering program in Canada.[5]

## Quick Facts about the University of Waterloo[6]

- The University has six faculties: Applied Health Science, Arts, Engineering, Environment, Mathematics and Science.

- University of Waterloo has four campuses Waterloo, Kitchener, Stratford and Cambridge.

- The University of Waterloo created the first Department of Kinesiology in the world.

- It has been ranked the most innovative university in Canada for 22 years by *Maclean's Magazine*.

- Thirty-two percent of graduate students are from outside of Canada.

- There are four colleges that are affiliated with the University of Waterloo they are: Conrad Grebel University College, St. Paul's University College, Renison University College, and St. Jerome's University.

- There are over 169,000 University of Waterloo alumni.

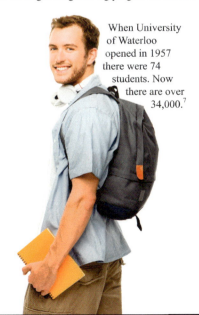

When University of Waterloo opened in 1957 there were 74 students. Now there are over 34,000.[7]

*Piece of History*

The above photograph is a back-to-class photograph from the University of Waterloo taken in October of 1965.

# FARMING & FOOD PROCESSING

Agriculture was the first industry that was established in Waterloo Region and it continues to thrive in the Region today. Complementing the farming sector, food processing has become a significant industry in Waterloo Region.

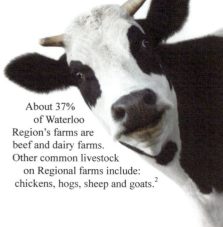

About 37% of Waterloo Region's farms are beef and dairy farms. Other common livestock on Regional farms include: chickens, hogs, sheep and goats.[2]

## FARMING

There are approximately 1,398 farms in Waterloo Region.[1] The farmland in Waterloo Region is some of the best in Ontario. The Region's farms are located in the townships.

There are many different crops grown in Waterloo Region including corn, wheat and soybeans.

Above is Steven and Rose Martin from Martin's Family Fruit Farm. Martin's is a successful local grower and distributor of apples and other fruits. The farm has been in the family since 1820.

### Living History

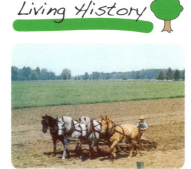

When pioneers first came to Waterloo Region, they used horses and oxen to help plow their fields.

Old Order Mennonites who choose not to use modern technology often still use many traditional farming methods, such as plows which are pulled by horses.

The image to the left, taken in 1950, is of an Old Order Mennonite farm in the Region.

There are

# 40

certified organic farms in Waterloo Region.[3]

"Agricultural land is still the dominant land use across the Region.

— Region of Waterloo Government[4]

## FOOD PROCESSING

Food processing is an important part of Waterloo Region's economy. There are many companies that create delicious foods within Waterloo Region including: JD Sweid Foods, Piller's Fine Foods, Weston Bakeries, Frito Lay and Dare Foods.

Dare Foods is a family-owned business which was founded, and is still headquartered, in Waterloo Region. It has many famous food brands such as Breton crackers and Bear Paw cookies. Dare has over 1,300 employees.[5]

### Piece of History

In 1857, Joseph Seagram founded a distillery in Waterloo Region. The company became the world-renown distillery Seagram Company. In the picture above, you can see a Seagram's production line. The Seagram Company has gone out of business, but some of its beverage brands were acquired by the Coca-Cola Company.

# BUSINESS
# MANUFACTURING

Waterloo Region has a diverse and successful manufacturing sector. The Region is well known for advanced manufacturing which uses sophisticated technology to build goods. Products that are manufactured in Waterloo Region range from cars to furniture.

Ontario Drive and Gear manufactures gears, transmissions and all terrain vehicles like the one seen here. The company was chosen to build a lunar rover.

## VEHICLES

Several vehicles are produced in Waterloo Region. By far the biggest producer of vehicles in the Region is Toyota. Toyota makes the Corolla and Lexus brand of cars in the City of Cambridge. In the Township of Wilmot, Ontario Drive and Gear produces all terrain vehicles. At the University of Waterloo, the Midnight Sun (see page 21) is a solar car that is designed, and continually improved, by university students.

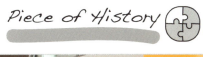
*Piece of History*

The LeRoy Car was produced in 1903 in the Town of Berlin, now the City of Kitchener. The car is on display at the Waterloo Region Museum. Production of the LeRoy stopped in 1904.

The first Toyota Corolla built in Cambridge is on display at Toyota's Visitor Centre in Cambridge. Toyota's Cambridge manufacturing facilities are very large, spanning approximately three million square feet.[1]

## OTHER MANUFACTURED ITEMS

Many different items are built in Waterloo Region. For example, some of the high-technology companies in the Region manufacture the products they design (see page 39); while Krug designs and manufactures furniture. For more local manufacturing companies, check out the table to the right.

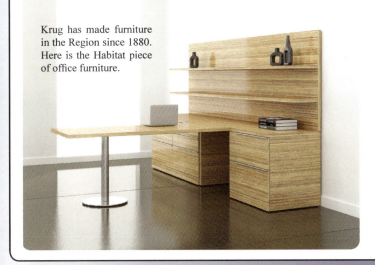

Krug has made furniture in the Region since 1880. Here is the Habitat piece of office furniture.

### More Manufacturing Companies in Waterloo Region

- **ATS Automation** designs and builds manufacturing systems.
- **Tenneco** produces automotive parts such as mufflers.
- **Kuntz Electroplating** specializes in chrome plating of metal items.
- **Lear Canada** produces automotive parts such as seating.
- **Sutherland-Shultz** produces sheet metal and other construction products.
- **Rockwell Automation Canada** makes machine and automation parts.

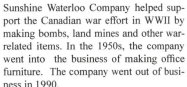
*Piece of History*

Sunshine Waterloo Company helped support the Canadian war effort in WWII by making bombs, land mines and other war-related items. In the 1950s, the company went into the business of making office furniture. The company went out of business in 1990.

This photo is of company employee Wib Karges working on the jig borer in the 1940s.[2]

# FINANCE

Waterloo Region has many businesses that create value in the finance industry. In particular, there are many successful insurance businesses located in Waterloo Region. Moreover, contributions to financial innovation have been made by local residents and companies.

## INSURANCE AND FINANCIAL SERVICES

Waterloo Region has a rich history in the insurance industry. Initially, farmers in the Region needed to protect themselves and their families financially if there was a fire or other serious event. So true to the Region's entrepreneurial history, local residents founded insurance companies to help farmers protect themselves in case of such a loss. Many of these insurance companies have been acquired or grown into large, modern insurance companies.

SunLife's Canadian head office is located in Waterloo, Canada. Sunlife has 7,815 employees in Canada.[2]

### Insurance Companies with Head Offices in the Region

**Economical Mutual Insurance Company:** Head office is in the City of Waterloo.

**Equitable Life Insurance Company of Canada:** Head office is in the City of Waterloo.

**Gore Mutual Insurance Company:** Head office is in the City of Cambridge.

**Manulife Financial:** Canadian division head office is in the City of Waterloo.

**H. L. Staebler Company:** Head office is in the City of Kitchener.

**North Waterloo Farmers Mutual Insurance Company:** Head office is in the City of Waterloo.

**SunLife Financial:** Canadian division head office is in the City of Waterloo.

Local universities offer training in accounting, actuarial science and business; so there are many skilled people to work in the Region's finance industry.

Waterloo Region resident David Chilton (born 1961) wrote the best-selling personal finance books *The Wealthy Barber* and *The Wealthy Barber Returns*.

*Piece of History*

The first mutual fire insurance company in Waterloo was the Waterloo Mutual Fire Insurance Company. The first insurance policies were issued in 1870. The building above was once owned by the company.[3]

## FINANCIAL INNOVATION

Research and development in the area of financial innovation is done in Waterloo Region. NCR has a research team located in Waterloo Region to develop and refine automated financial transactions. There is also the Centre of International Governance Innovation which has researchers who consider financial policy issues. Moreover, both local universities have a department of economics with professors who research economic issues.

The Centre of International Governance Innovation (CIGI), founded by local entrepreneur James Basillie, brings together leading thinkers on a broad range of issues including global finance. To the left is an image of a conference at CIGI.

Susan Carreon of NCR's research facility in Waterloo Region is standing beside an Automated Teller Machine (ATM) that her team developed. This machine allows people to directly deposit cash and cheques without using an envelope.

# HOSPITALITY & SERVICES

There is a great hospitality industry in Waterloo Region which helps residents and visitors have fun and relax. There are also many other services, beyond hospitality, that are provided by Waterloo Region businesses which help residents meet their day-to-day needs.

FunWorX is a large indoor playground in Kitchener where kids can play, climb and have fun all year. FunWorX is part of Bingemans, one of the Region's largest hospitality providers.

## HOSPITALITY

There is a wonderful selection of places to stay and things to do in Waterloo Region; and behind these great experiences are highly-capable businesses.

In the Region, there are hospitality businesses that provide experiences ranging from indoor rock climbing to golf. There are also many prosperous restaurants and hotels.

In 1893, for

# $4.50

a person could stay one week at a local hotel.[1]

**#1** Waterloo Region hotel Langdon Hall was voted best hotel in Canada by Conde Naste.[2]

Langdon Hall was built by Eugene Langdon Wilks in 1902. It was used as a summer home by his family and descendants until 1980. In 1987, the home was bought by William Bennett and Mary Beaton. They transformed the building into a world-renown hotel.

There are many lovely restaurants in the Region from great pizza places to fine dining.

## MORE SERVICES

There are a broad range of services that regional businesses offer. There are many professional services such as lawyers and accountants; transportation services including taxies, private cars, and limousines; home repair services for any part of your home; and personal services including hair cuts, manicures and more.

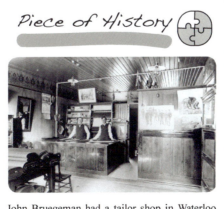

*Piece of History*

John Bruegeman had a tailor shop in Waterloo from about 1890 to 1950. In this picture of his shop, Mr. Bruegeman is on the left and his assistant on the right.[3]

There are many repair and construction services available in the Region.

# TECHNOLOGY

Waterloo Region has a dynamic technology sector. The technology industry in the Region is fuelled by many factors. First, there are many residents with great math, engineering or business skills because of their education at local universities and colleges. Second, there are many organizations that help entrepreneurs establish and grow their new technology businesses. And third, there is a great support network for people who choose to start their own companies.

## TECHNOLOGY ENTREPRENEURSHIP

Technology entrepreneurship is rigorously supported in Waterloo Region. Organizations, such as Communitech, support new technology companies with a broad range of services such as connecting entrepreneurs with mentors. Several local organizations, such as the Accelerator Centre, offer technology companies access to economical office space and specialized business services. There are also many entrepreneurship-friendly policies and education streams offered by the local universities.

Mike Lazaridis (born 1961) is Waterloo Region's most famous technology entrepreneur. He founded the technology company Research In Motion, now called Blackberry. Mr. Lazaridis is also a very generous philanthropist, and a promoter of science education and research. He is the founder of the Perimeter Institute which is a place dedicated to the study of theoretical physics.

Students can take courses in entrepreneurship and have access to other business support services while in school. Graduates of the local universities often choose to start their own technology company or to work for a start-up technology company when they graduate.

Waterloo Region has great resources for establishing new technology companies including business support services for entrepreneurs, an Accelerator Centre, and a supportive start-up community.

### Piece of History

One factor that helped cultivate high-technological entrepreneurship in Waterloo Region is that the University of Waterloo adopted a very simple intellectual property policy. The policy allows professors and students to keep all the rights to their research and inventions. The benefits of this policy to the University of Waterloo, and Waterloo Region, were several fold. First, it helped attract very talented professors to the University of Waterloo. Second, it gave professors every incentive to maximize and commercialize any advances in research they made, because they could keep the profits. Not surprisingly, this has lead to many high-technology companies being started by university professors.

The Communitech Hub is a place where technology companies can get start-up office space. There is also a large space for local technology presentations and networking meetings.

# TECHNOLOGY COMPANIES

There are many technology companies in Waterloo Region. In fact, Communitech estimates there are almost one thousand.[1] Many technology companies were started in the Region including: Blackberry, OpenText and Desire2Learn. Larger technology companies from other parts of the world have also opened offices in Waterloo Region because of the large talent pool of potential employees in the Region, examples of such companies include Google and Square.

The Blackberry® smartphone is developed and manufactured by Waterloo company Blackberry (formerly Research in Motion). The Blackberry company is one of the biggest technology companies in Canada.

Google and the Google logo are registered trademarks of Google Inc. used with permission.

Google is a great example of one of the many large technology companies which have opened an office in Waterloo Region because of the highly-skilled workforce and dynamic technology sector.

There are almost

# 1,000

technology firms in Waterloo Region.[2]

There are several application development companies in the Region. For example, Kik is a company that created messaging software which is used by more than 100 million people.[3]

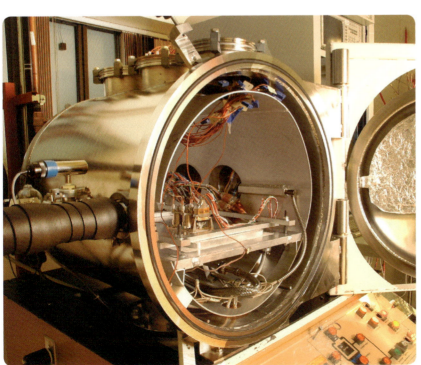

COM DEV is a technology company that specializes in space engineering. The company builds and designs space systems like the satellite seen to the left. In fact, COM DEV is the largest satellite company in Canada.

## More Technology Companies

**OpenText** is the largest software company in Canada. It provides information management software to businesses.

**Desire2Learn** is a successful e-learning company.

**Christie Digital Systems** designs and produces digital display systems.

**Descartes Systems Group** designs logistics and mobile applications.

**Sandvine** develops technology to help broadband networks work more efficiently.

**Aeryon Labs** designs and develops small, unmanned robots that can fly.

**Teledyne Dalsa** designs and makes image sensors.

**Maluuba** creates computer applications that integrate natural language processing.

**Peer Group** develops automation software for manufacturing.

**Coreworx** makes software to manage gas and oil projects.

**Rebellion Media** is an integrated digital media company.

**Igloo** creates social media software for companies.

# ON THE FIELD

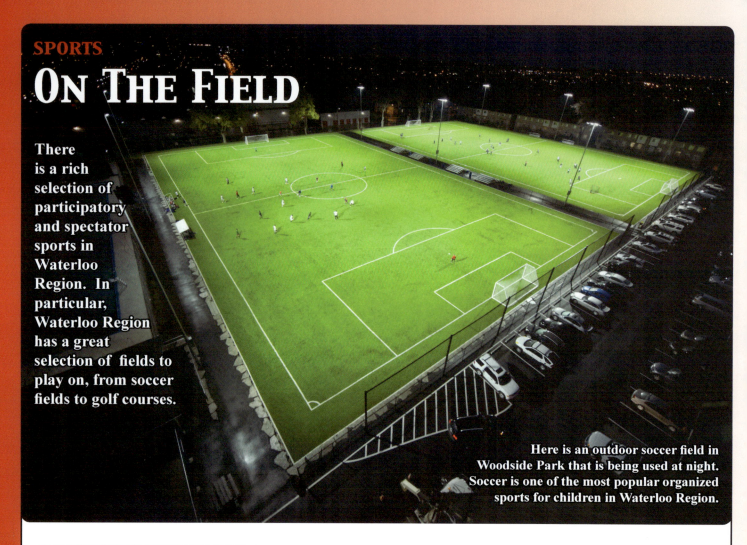

There is a rich selection of participatory and spectator sports in Waterloo Region. In particular, Waterloo Region has a great selection of fields to play on, from soccer fields to golf courses.

Here is an outdoor soccer field in Woodside Park that is being used at night. Soccer is one of the most popular organized sports for children in Waterloo Region.

Professional golf player Hee Young Park, above, is chipping at the 18th green at the Manulife Financial LPGA Classic. This tournament was held at the Grey Silo Golf Course located at RIM Park in Waterloo Region, in the City of Waterloo. There are many exceptional public and private golf courses in the Region.

## Some Field Sports Played in Waterloo Region

| |
| --- |
| Lawn bowling |
| Field hockey |
| Golf |
| Baseball |
| Softball |
| Football |
| Cricket |
| Track and field |
| Paintball |
| Soccer |
| Horseshoe pitching |
| And more |

Football is a popular field sport in Waterloo Region.

## Great Athelete

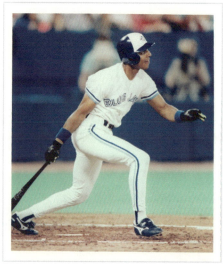

Professional baseball player Rob Ducey (born 1965) was born in Waterloo Region, in the City of Cambridge. His professional baseball career started in 1984. Mr. Ducey played an impressive 19 years of professional baseball. He played for several teams including the Toronto Blue Jays, Montreal Expos and Texas Rangers.

# ON THE ICE & SNOW

There are many sports that are played on snow or ice in Waterloo Region during the winter months. Some winter sports, such as hockey, can be played all year because of the high-quality, four-season arenas that are available in Waterloo Region. While other sports such as skiing and sledding are done in the Region only during the winter.

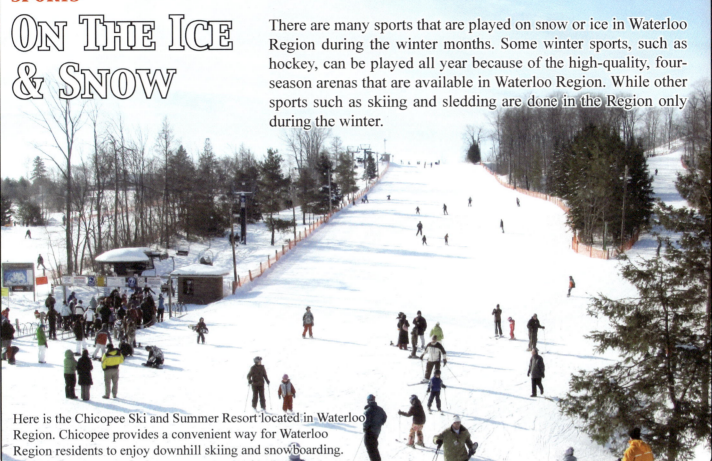

Here is the Chicopee Ski and Summer Resort located in Waterloo Region. Chicopee provides a convenient way for Waterloo Region residents to enjoy downhill skiing and snowboarding.

Hockey is one of the most popular sports in Waterloo Region. There are arenas and hockey teams across the Region for players of all ages and ability levels. Watching hockey is also popular. In particular, the Kitchener Rangers draw large crowds to their hockey games at the Kitchener Memorial Auditorium.

Curling is popular in the Region. There are several curling clubs including the Ayr Curling Club, Elmira and District Curling Club, and the KW Granite Club.

**Preston Figure Skating Club of Cambridge**

Saturday March 23, 2013
Preston Memorial Auditorium
Shows at 2:00 pm and 7:00 pm
For ticket information call!
(519) 653-2252 or visit
www.prestonfsc.com
Silent auction at the event

There are several figure skating clubs in the Region. The Preston Figure Skating Club puts on a lovely, annual skating show with all levels of skaters.

### Some of the Waterloo Region's Snow and Ice Sports

| | |
|---|---|
| Cross-country skiing | Hockey |
| Snowshoeing | Figure skating |
| Curling | Hiking |
| Ringette | Sledding |
| Tubing | Downhill skiing |
| Snowboarding | Speed skating |

### Great Athelete

Kelly VanderBeek (born 1983) started to downhill ski competitively with the Chicopee Ski Club when she was eight years old. She competed on the World Cup Tour and in the Olympics in 2006.

# IN THE WATER

Many water sports can be enjoyed in Waterloo Region. Water sports that need to be done outdoors, such as boating and fishing, are engaged in mostly during the warmer months. While other water sports, such as swimming, can be enjoyed year-round because of the many indoor pools available in the Region.

Laurel Creek Conservation Area, seen above, has areas for swimming and boating. There are several conservation areas in the Region which are administered by the Grand River Conservation Authority.

## Great Athelete

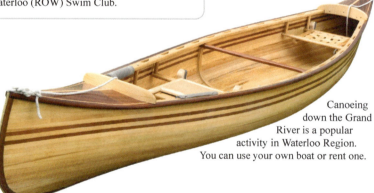

Victor Davis (1964–1989) won an Olympic gold medal in 1984 for the 200 meter breast stroke. He also won two silver medals during the same Olympics. Victor Davis trained at the Region of Waterloo (ROW) Swim Club.

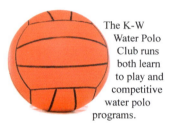

The K-W Water Polo Club runs both learn to play and competitive water polo programs.

| Some of Waterloo Region's Water Sports | |
|---|---|
| Water polo | Kayaking |
| Canoeing | Rowing |
| Fishing | Diving |
| Water aerobics | Synchronized swimming |
| Swimming | And more |

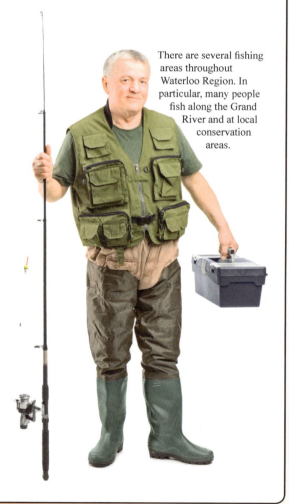

There are several fishing areas throughout Waterloo Region. In particular, many people fish along the Grand River and at local conservation areas.

Canoeing down the Grand River is a popular activity in Waterloo Region. You can use your own boat or rent one.

Swimming lessons are available in Waterloo Region for people of all ages. There are also many public swimming pools which offer public, family and lane swims; as well as pool rentals.

# On The Court, In The Gym & More

Tennis courts can be found throughout Waterloo Region. There are tennis courts in community parks that are free to play on. There are also several private tennis clubs in the Region.

There are many great sports that are played on the courts, and in gymnasiums, of Waterloo Region. In particular, sports such as basketball, volleyball and tennis are popular. Regional residents can play in parks, community centres, and in private or specialized facilities.

### Great Athelete

Sherry (Hawco) Delanty (1964–1991) was a Canadian Gymnastics Champion in 1979 and 1980; and qualified for the Olympics. She trained with the Cambridge Kips.

The Stanley Park Community Centre is an example of one of the many community centres in Waterloo Region where there are easily accessible gym sports.

Volleyball is a popular sport in schools, community centres and competitive leagues.

Table tennis is popular sport in residents' homes and at local clubs in Waterloo Region.

| Some of Waterloo Region's Sports Played on Courts, in Gyms and More | |
|---|---|
| Squash | Table tennis |
| Boxing | Gymnastics |
| Aerobics | Floor hockey |
| Badminton | Racquetball |
| Volleyball | Basketball |
| Judo | Wrestling |

### Great Athelete

Lennox Lewis (born 1965) won a gold medal in the 1988 Olympic Games. In 1993, he became an Undisputed Heavy Weight Champion of the World.

Mr. Lewis moved to Waterloo Region when he was twelve. He lived in Kitchener. When in high school, Mr. Lewis attended Cameron Heights Collegiate.

There are several basketball leagues in the Region. There are also community centre basketball lessons, and basketball summer camps. Many parks also have basketball hoops for impromptu games.

# VISUAL ARTS

The visual arts thrive in Waterloo Region. In fact, many famous visual artists came from the Region. There are also many local galleries where Waterloo Region residents can go to enjoy both local and international artists' work. Moreover, there are many opportunities for anyone to cultivate their artistic skills.

Homer Watson (1855–1936) is Waterloo Region's most famous artist. He spent most of his life painting Waterloo Region's countryside, such as the painting seen above. Some of Homer Watson paintings are in the Queen of England's collection. His former home, in Kitchener, is now a gallery and a place where students can take art lessons.

## LOCAL ART AND ARTISTS

There are many local visual artists who have been very successful within the Region and abroad, such as Carl Ahrens and Homer Watson.

Carl Ahrens (1862–1936) is one of the Region's most successful painters. He attended school in the Region before travelling and painting abroad. Mr. Ahrens was an impressionist painter.

### Metamorphosis

was the winner of the Palme d'Or for Best Short Film at the prestigious Cannes International Film Festival. The film was made by Barry Greenwald who is a graduate of Conestoga College.

Jane Buyers is a current artist and professor in Waterloo Region. To the left is her work *Book of Hours IV*.

Florence Carlyle (1864–1923) was born in Waterloo Region. Her paintings have been widely shown. To the left is her painting *The Tiff*.

## LEARNING

There are many places to learn how to paint, sculpt and do other visual arts in the Region. Residents can take art courses at Conestoga College, several community centres, the Button Factory, and the Homer Watson House and Gallery.

The Canadian Clay and Glass Gallery located in the City of Waterloo has clay sculpting activities for families.

Living History

The Waterloo Community Arts Centre is a place where artists gather, take workshops and display their art. The building originally housed the Roschman and Brother Button Company from 1886 to 1940; this is why the arts centre is commonly know as The Button Factory.

## VIEWING

Art in Waterloo Region is easy to find. Some of the places to see visual art in the Region include:

- Kitchener-Waterloo Art Gallery;
- The Rotunda Gallery;
- The Button Factory;
- Cambridge Libraries and Galleries;
- Cambridge Sculpture Garden;
- CAFKA Public Art Display;
- St. Jacobs Quilt Gallery;
- Neufeld Gallery;
- Homer Watson House and Gallery;
- University of Waterloo Art Gallery;
- Canadian Clay and Glass Gallery;
- and the Uptown Gallery.

# THE ARTS
# MUSIC

There is a vibrant music scene in Waterloo Region. Many great musicians have come from this area. While residents have the opportunity to enjoy music festivals and individual performances throughout the year. For people who would like to learn more about music, there are many music lessons and courses available in the Region.

The Kitchener-Waterloo Symphony is a local symphony, with international acclaim, that was founded in 1945 by Dr. Glenn Kruspe. The symphony plays across the Region, including at the Centre In The Square.

## LOCAL MUSICIANS

Many residents and former residents of Waterloo Region have become very successful in a wide variety of music genres.

Born in Kitchener, Danny Michel (born 1970) is an accomplished musician with ten released albums and other musical projects.

Erick Traplin (born 1949) is a children's entertainer who has released several CDs and books. Mr. Traplin often performs in Waterloo Region.

Opera singer Jane Archibald studied music at Wilfrid Laurier University. She won a Juno for her first CD.

Award-winning blues musician Steve Strongman grew up in the City of Kitchener. Strongman is an accomplished songwriter, guitarist and vocalist.

## LEARNING

There are many places to learn music skills in Waterloo Region. Music classes range from group classes at local community centres to private instruction with professional music teachers. For people who are interested in becoming professional musicians, Wilfrid Laurier University has one of Canada's top music training programs.

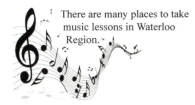

There are many places to take music lessons in Waterloo Region.

Piece of History

The Waterloo Musical Society Band, pictured above, was founded in 1882. The band played in many festivals and won several awards. It also played, for many years, annually at the Canadian National Exhibition.

## ENJOYING

Enjoying music is easy in Waterloo Region. There are many places to catch a live musical performance in the Region including the Centre In The Square, the Conrad Centre for the Performing Arts, and several restaurants and bars. There are also several live music festivals in the Region every year. Below is a list of some of the festivals.

| Waterloo Region Music Festivals |
| --- |
| Kitchener Waterloo Kiwanis Music Festival |
| Uptown Country Waterloo Music Festival |
| Kitchener Blues Festival |
| New Hamburg Live |

# THEATER & DRAMATIC ARTS

Whether you want to see a dramatic play or a light-hearted comedy, there are many wonderful places in Waterloo Region to take in a live theatre performance. Residents also have many opportunities to learn more about the theatre.

Jill Hennessy (born 1968) lived in Waterloo Region, attending Kitchener's Grand River Collegiate Institute. She has starred in two hit TV shows: *Law & Order* and *Crossing Jordan*. She has also been in several movies.

## LOCAL PERFORMERS AND SHOWS

Catching a live show is easy in Waterloo Region. Several theatre companies in the Region produce live performances including:

* Lost and Found Theatre;
* JM Drama;
* Drayton Entertainment;
* Kitchener Waterloo Little Theatre;
* Cambridge Community Players;
* Kitchener Waterloo Musical Productions; and
* Multicultural Theatre Space.

These groups can choose to perform in one of the many different theatres in the Region. Most of these theatre companies also use talented performers who reside in the Region in their performances.

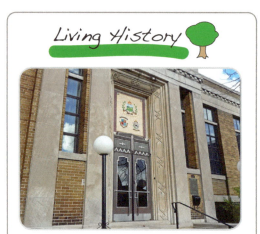

Here are Mark Ledbetter, Jayme Armstrong and the Cast of Mary Poppins at the Dunfield Theatre in Cambridge. The theatre was built by Drayton Entertainment, which is a company that produces popular plays and musicals across the Region, and in other Ontario venues.

## LEARNING

There are many places that you can learn about performing and acting in Waterloo Region. There are summer camps and courses for children who are interested in performing in live theatre. Several of the local community theatre companies also hold auditions for local actors to participate in their productions. The University of Waterloo has a drama department for serious theatre students.

There are many places to learn about the theatre in Waterloo Region.

### Living History

The Registry Theatre is a beautiful historic building with a theatre space that is operated by the theatre company JM Drama. It was originally built in 1939 to be the Waterloo Country Registry Office. In 2001, it was repurposed as a theatre.

## ENJOYING

Residents can enjoy a theater performance at many different theatres in the Region including:

* St. Jacobs Country Playhouse Theatre;
* University of Waterloo Theatre Centre;
* Dunfield Theatre;
* Centre In The Square;
* Conrad Centre for the Performing Arts; and
* Stage One.

While many productions are local, internationally acclaimed shows also come to the Region, usually performing at the Centre In The Square.

# THE ARTS
# WRITING

Many successful professional writers and publishers have ties to Waterloo Region. People who would like to cultivate their writing skills can take part in classes and groups that are held in the Region. And most importantly, in Waterloo Region it is very easy to access great writing through local libraries, schools, online and at local bookstores.

Malcolm Gladwell (born 1963) is an author of four best-selling books including *The Tipping Point* and *Blink*. He grew up in Waterloo Region in the Town of Elmira; and his father was a professor at the University of Waterloo.

## LOCAL WRITERS AND PUBLISHERS

Many accomplished fiction and non-fiction writers have a meaningful connection to Waterloo Region including Malcolm Gladwell, Edna Staebler and David Morrell.

John B. Crozier (1849–1922) lived in Waterloo Region and later moved to Britain. He wrote the successful philosophy book *Civilization and Progress*.[1]

Margaret Millar (1915–1994) was a famous mystery writer who was born in Kitchener. She wrote many novels including *The Invisible Worm* and *Beast in View.*

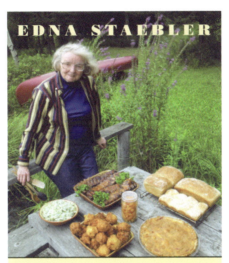

EDNA STAEBLER

**Schmecks Appeal**

More Mennonite Country Cooking

Edna Staebler (1906–2006) was a prolific writer in the area of creative non-fiction. Three of her books combined Mennonite recipes with short stories and anecdotes. Edna Staebler was awarded the Order of Canada in 1996.

### Waterloo Region Publishers and Periodicals

**Wilfrid Laurier Press** is an academic press that publishes in areas of history, politics and other social issues.

**Volumes Publishing** is a self-publishing press that helps bring authors' work into print.

**The New Quarterly** is a literary journal which focuses on publishing fiction and poetry.

**Many magazines** are published in the Region including *Grand Magazine*, *Most Magazine* and *Canadian Skies Magazine*.

David Morrell (born 1943) wrote the novel *First Blood* which was turned into the *Rambo* film franchise. Mr. Morrell was born in Kitchener, although he later moved to the United States. He has published many books since his debut novel.

## LEARNING

Writing is a popular activity in Waterloo Region, and it is reflected in the many opportunities offered to learn the craft. There are a broad range of writing courses available in the Region at local libraries, grade schools, colleges and universities.

Joint Ventures

One Book, One Community

Each year Waterloo Region residents are encouraged to read the same book as part of the "One Book, One Community" program. The program includes special events where people can gather and discuss the book, or even meet the author.[2]

## ENJOYING

Bookstores, libraries, schools, and community centres are just some of the places where residents can get books and magazines. Also, Waterloo Region has exceptional internet access throughout the community which can be helpful when trying to quickly download ebooks online.

# PREVENTING ILLNESS

Healthy lifestyle options are readily available in Waterloo Region. There is a wide variety of fresh food that can be purchased in the Region; as well as many opportunities for physical activity. Moreover, the Region of Waterloo's Public Health Department runs many health promotion programs to help residents of the Region stay healthy.

There are many places in Waterloo Region where residents can participate in exercise classes including fitness clubs, community centres and specialized locations such as yoga studios.

## HEALTH CULTIVATION

Fresh, healthy food can be bought at local farmers' markets, as well as local grocery stores. There are many restaurants that try to offer healthy food options. Many opportunities to exercise are also available in the Region including: sports clubs, exercise classes and outdoor activities.

Fresh vegetables are available at farmers' markets and local grocery stores.

Sledding is just one of the many outdoor activities that Waterloo Region's residents can enjoy to recharge and feel good.

### Health Leader 💗

Lyle Hallman (1922–2003) was a successful real estate developer who gave generously to his community to help cultivate healthy living. Mr. Hallman founded the Lyle S. Hallman Foundation which has supported many healthy living initiatives in Waterloo Region such as the Lyle Hallman Institute for Health Promotion, and several programs that work to promote healthy development in children.

## WELLNESS PROMOTION PROGRAMS

The Region of Waterloo Public Health Department works hard to help improve the health of Waterloo Region residents. The department provides a wealth of health information and a broad range of specialized programs for community residents.

The Region of Waterloo Public Health Department puts a great deal of health information online.

Vaccinations for diseases such as chickenpox are available through the Region's health clinics and nurses.

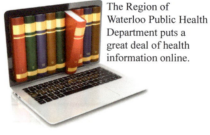

Keeping teeth healthy is supported by local dentists and public health programs. Dental hygienists come into schools to make sure that children are receiving dental health support.

### More Waterloo Region Public Health Promotion Activities [1]

- Promoting cancer screening and behaviours that can reduce the risk of cancer.

- Inspecting places which prepare food and providing training programs for people who prepare food for sale.

- Inspecting places that provide beauty and body art services.

- Providing programs that promote healthy eating for all age groups.

- Child Health Fairs that bring many health providers together for families.

- Inspecting small drinking water systems for water quality.

- Prenatal Health Fairs that provide expecting mothers with a broad range of resources.

# HEALTH
# TREATING ILLNESS

Unfortunately, sometimes people get sick. In Waterloo Region, there are many physicians, nurses and other health care professionals who work to help people heal and feel better. Training programs for individuals who want to work in the health care sector are also available in the Region.

## PATIENT CARE

A wide variety of personal health treatment solutions are available to local residents. If someone is feeling ill, they can visit their family doctor, a walk-in clinic, or if it is more serious, a hospital emergency room. Patients are often referred to specialists in particular diseases. If needed, there are three hospitals in the Region which provide advanced treatment for a wide-range of illnesses.

There are also many other health care providers in the Region including physiotherapists, optometrists, and occupational therapists, just to name a few. Alternative health professionals such as chiropractors and naturopathic doctors also practice in the Region.

## TREATMENT TRAINING

There are several schools located within Waterloo Region that train health professionals. This helps maintain a good ratio of health professionals to residents in the Region, as many health professionals choose to work in the Region in which they were trained.

There are several hospitals in the Region including the Cambridge Memorial Hospital, St. Mary's General Hospital and Grand River Hospital (GRH). GRH has several locations including: GRH Freeport Site, GRH Kitchener-Waterloo Site, and several smaller locations with specialized services.

### Health Leader ♥

Charles Miller Fisher (1913–2012) was born in Waterloo, Ontario. He went to high school at Kitchener-Waterloo Collegiate. Dr. Fisher became a world famous neurologist, and a member of the Canadian Medical Hall of Fame. Dr. Fisher was particularly known for his work regarding the causes, and methods of preventing, strokes.

The School of Pharmacy, which is part of the University of Waterloo, is located in downtown Kitchener.

### Some Health Education Programs in Waterloo Region

**University of Waterloo.** This school's health programs include: the School of Pharmacy which trains pharmacists; and the School of Optometry which trains optometrists.

**Conestoga College.** Many health care programs are offered by the college's School of Health & Life Sciences and Community Services including: Respiratory Therapy, Applied Health Information Science, Practical Nursing, Personal Support Worker and Hearing Instrument Specialist.

**McMaster University.** This Hamilton-based university's Faculty of Health Sciences provides education at its Waterloo Regional Campus for an Undergraduate Medical Program to become a physician; and its School of Nursing offers a Bachelor of Science in Nursing Program at Conestoga College.

**Career Colleges.** Several smaller career colleges, like Medix College of Health Care, offer health care programs such as Personal Support Worker and Pharmacy Assistant.

# CITY OF CAMBRIDGE

The City of Cambridge is the second largest city in Waterloo Region. It was formed in 1973 by putting together the City of Galt, the Town of Preston, the Town of Hespeler, and the Village of Blair. This unusual amalgamation resulted in the City of Cambridge having three charming downtown areas. Cambridge also has two lovely rivers, many parks and the Shade's Mill Conservation Area.

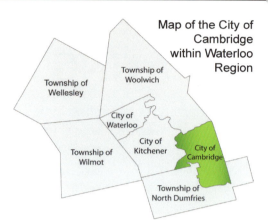

Map of the City of Cambridge within Waterloo Region

Township of Wellesley
Township of Woolwich
City of Waterloo
City of Kitchener
Township of Wilmot
City of Cambridge
Township of North Dumfries

## LAYOUT OF THE CITY

There are many residential, business and natural spaces throughout the City of Cambridge. The Speed River runs past the Hespeler downtown area in the northern part of the City; while the Grand River runs past the Galt downtown area in the southern part of the City. In the west area of Cambridge, the two rivers merge and you find the Preston section of the City which also has its own downtown area.

**North**

In the northeastern part of Cambridge is the Hespeler area. This area includes a charming downtown with shops and historic buildings. You will also find many residential areas and the Speed River. In the northwestern part of the City, there is the Cambridge Butterfly Conservatory and Toyota's manufacturing facilities.

**East**

This area is a mix of residential homes and industrial areas zoned for businesses. There is also the Shade's Mill Conservation Area which is run by the Grand River Conservation Authority. The conservation area has a lake for swimming and boating.

*Map labels:*
Silver Heights · Mill Pond · Cambridge Butterfly Conservatory · Hespeler Village · Business & Industrial Area · Hespeler Downtown · Popcorn House · Toyota Plant · Speed River · Highway 401 · Business & Industrial Area · Fiddlesticks · Langs Farm · Preston Heights · Preston Downtown · Preston Centre · Greenway Chaplin · Shade's Mill Reservior · Rare Charitable Research Reserve · Whistle Bear Golf Course · Galt Golf & Country Club · Dumfries Conservation Area · Shade's Mill Conservation Area · Cambridge Memorial Hospital · Blair Road · East Galt · Alison · Grand River · Galt Downtown · Kinbridge · Cambridge Sculpture Garden

North / West · East / South

### West and Central

This area of Cambridge is often called Preston. In this area, there is a charming downtown and several residential communities. The Speed River and the Grand River merge together here. Also, the Rare Charitable Research Reserve is in this area.

**Legend**

| | | | |
|---|---|---|---|
| Downtown Area | H Hospital | | River or Lake |
| Golf Course | Park or Natural Area | | Highway |
| Residential Area | Business or Industrial Area | | |

Note: This map is not to scale, it is for general information purposes only.

### South

South Cambridge is often called Galt. Galt's rich Scottish history is evident in the classic stone architecture of downtown Galt. The Grand River runs through Galt. Along the Grand River's banks, there is a beautiful sculpture garden. Also in Galt, you can find the City's main library branch called the Queen's Square Library, and Cambridge City Hall. There are also many stores, offices and residential areas.

## Quick Facts

**People:**
- Population of 132,900;[1]
- 47,700 households;[2]
- Median age is 38 years old;[3]
- Primary language spoken at home is English, second is Portuguese, third is Panjabi.[4]

**Land:**
- Size of the City is 113 kilometers squared;[5]
- Density is 1,176 people per kilometer squared;[6]
- Highway 401 goes through the City;
- Speed River in the north and the Grand River in the south.

**Employment and industry:**
- Toyota, the car manufacturer, is the largest employer in the City of Cambridge;[7]
- Over 25% of the Cambridge workforce is employed in manufacturing.[8]

**Community amenities:**[9]
- 12 community centres;
- 4 public library branches;
- 16 soccer fields;
- 7 ice surfaces;
- 5 indoor and 4 outdoor pools.

## Name Meaning

The Cambridge name came from Prince George, Duke of Cambridge (1819–1904), seen below. However, the story of the use of his name is a little complicated. Before the Town of Preston was called Preston, it was

known as Cambridge Mills after the Duke. The name of Cambridge Mills was later changed to Preston. But in 1973, when the communities of Preston, Hespeler, Galt, and Blair were put together, officials brought back the Cambridge name.

# NOTABLE RESIDENTS

The City of Cambridge has had many distinguished residents. For example, Rob Ducey is a famous baseball player from Cambridge who played for the Toronto Blue Jays (see page 40). Two other notable residents include pioneer Jacob Hespeler and former Mayor of Preston, and the City of Cambridge, Claudette Millar.

Jacob Hespeler (1810–1881) came to the Preston part of Cambridge in 1835 where he became a store owner. He then moved to the New Hope area, later called Hespeler in his honour.

Claudette Millar became the first Mayor of Cambridge in 1973. She was 35 years old which made her the youngest mayor in Canada at the time. Prior to that, she was the Mayor of Preston.

# INTERESTING PLACES

There are many unique places in the City of Cambridge. There are museums such as McDougall Cottage (see page 10) and the Cambridge Fire Museum. There are also many beautiful historic buildings throughout the City of Cambridge.

The City of Cambridge has several natural areas such as the Shade's Mill Conservation Area, Churchill Park and Riverside Park. Moreover, there are two lovely rivers that run through the City, the Speed River and the Grand River.

To the left is the old Hespeler Town Hall which was built from 1914–1915. The building is now the home of the Hespeler Heritage Centre.

The Speed and Grand Rivers come to together in the Preston area of Cambridge. There are lovely trails by these rivers.

Living History

This floor mill located in the Preston area of Cambridge is the longest running flour mill in the Region. It has operated continuously since 1879, although the ownership of the mill has changed during this time.

The downtown area in the Galt section of Cambridge is known for its beautiful stone buildings and lovely architecture.

Sheaves Tower was built to power a flour mill around 1876. The tower has been restored and is now a beautiful landmark in the western part of Cambridge.

The Cambridge Butterfly Conservatory has thousands of free-flying butterflies for patrons to see within an indoor tropical garden.

# SPECIAL EVENTS

Residents can enjoy many events and festivals in the City of Cambridge including the Cambridge Highland Games and the Cambridge Fall Fair. The Cambridge Public Libraries and Galleries also host several special events. Cambridge has several parades including the Christmas Parade and the Portugal Day Parade.

The Cambridge Mill Race Festival is a folk music festival. Here you can see a evening performance in the downtown Galt area of Cambridge.

# CITY OF KITCHENER

The City of Kitchener is the largest city in Waterloo Region. Kitchener has many significant resources including hospitals, art galleries, museums, sports facilities and theatres. People from across the Region will often come to the City of Kitchener to take advantage of the wide range of amenities, making the City of Kitchener a very busy place.

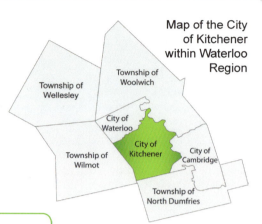

Map of the City of Kitchener within Waterloo Region

## LAYOUT OF THE CITY

Kitchener's downtown is quite dense with many stores, office buildings, cultural places and residential buildings; while the areas outside the downtown are less dense, they are filled with residential areas, businesses and parks. In addition, the Grand River is on the east side of Kitchener; and there is a highway which loops through the City which makes getting around Kitchener by car convenient.

### Central

There are four sections to Kitchener's Downtown including: City Centre, Civic District, Warehouse District and Market District. The City Centre section includes Kitchener City Hall, a museum, a performing arts centre, and many stores and offices. The Civic District includes the KPL Central Library, the Centre In The Square, and the KW Art Gallery. The Market District has the Kitchener Market and other stores. Finally, the Warehouse District has several old factories, such as the Lang Tannery, that have been converted into high-tech business offices. There are also residential condominiums that were originally factories.

### North

North Kitchener is made up mainly of residential areas. It also has the Woodside National Historic Site and some well-developed commercial areas. Kiwanis Park is also located in this area.

### West

West Kitchener is home to the largest natural area in Kitchener, Huron Natural Area. There are also many established residential areas such as Forest Heights and Forest Hill in this area.

**Map labels:**
Kiwanis Park
Bridgeport North
Bridgeport East
Business & Industrial Area
Grand River
Highway 85
Woodside Historic Site
Rosemount & Heritage Park
Bingemans
GR Hospital KW Site
Warehouse District
Grand River North
Westmount Country Club
Victoria Hills
Civic District
City Centre
Stanley Park & Idlewood
Beechwood West
Joseph Schneider Haus
Market District
Rockway Golf Course
Grand River South
Chicopee Ski Hill
St. Mary's Hospital
GR Hospital Freeport Site
Highland West
Forest Heights
Forest Hill
Rockway & Kingsdale Area
Deer Ridge Golf Course
Pioneer Tower West
Pioneer Tower
Doon Valley Golf Course
Highway 7/8
Laurentian Hills
Country Hills
Waterloo Region Museum
Highway 401
Laurentian West
Business & Industrial Area
Conestoga College
Huron Natural Area
Brigadoon
Pioneer Park
Lower Doon
Residential area under development

Compass:
North
West East
South

### South

The southern area of Kitchener has Conestoga College, the Waterloo Region Museum and several residential areas. There is significant new home construction in the southwest area of Kitchener.

### East

The Grand River is located in the eastern part of Kitchener. Situated by the river are lovely walking trails. There is also Bingemans, and Chicopee Ski and Summer Resort, in this area. Several residential areas are located in the east part of Kitchener.

### Legend

- Downtown Area
- Hospital (H)
- River or Lake
- Golf Course
- Park or Natural Area
- Highway
- Residential Area
- Business or Industrial Area

Note: This map is not to scale, it is for general information purposes only.

## Quick Facts

**People:**
- Population of 232,000;[1]
- 88,210 households;[2]
- Median age is 37.2 years old;[3]
- Primary language spoken at home is English, second is German, and third is Spanish.[4]

**Land:**
- Size of Kitchener is 136.79 kilometers squared;[5]
- Density is 1,696 people per kilometer squared;[6]
- The Grand River runs along the east side of the City.

**Employment and industry:**[7]
- Manulife Financial and Dare Foods are the top private employers in the city;
- There are 498 acres of business parks in the City.

**Community amenities:**[8]
- 15 community centres;
- 4 indoor pools and 3 outdoor public pools;
- 220 parks and over 125 kilometers of walking trails;
- 5 indoor arenas and many outdoor ice surfaces.

## Name Meaning

The City of Kitchener got its name from Britian's Lord Horatio Herbert Kitchener (1860–1915) who became Secretary State for War at the beginning of the First World War, in 1914. He died halfway through this war. Above is an illustration of Lord Kitchener which was included in an army recruitment poster.

# NOTABLE RESIDENTS

William Lyon Mackenzie King was Canada's longest serving Prime Minister and is the most famous person to have lived in the City of Kitchener.

Other famous former residents include CTV news anchor Lisa LaFlamme, actress Jill Hennessy (see page 46), artist Homer Watson (see page 44), and boxing champion Lennox Lewis (see page 43).

William Lyon Mackenzie King (1874–1950) is Canada's longest serving Prime Minister. He was born in Kitchener, then named Berlin, and spent his childhood in the Region.

Lisa LaFlamme (born 1964) is the anchor of CTV National News. She was born and grew up in the City of Kitchener. Ms. LaFlamme started her career at the local Kitchener affiliate of CTV which was then called CKCO.

# INTERESTING PLACES

The City of Kitchener has many unique places. There are several museums including: the Waterloo Region Museum (see page 65), Joseph Schneider Haus (see page 10), and Woodside National Historic Site.

You can find many beautiful parks in the City of Kitchener from the flower-rich Rockway Park to the forested Huron Natural Area.

Kitchener has many other recreational places such as Chicopee Ski and Summer Resort (see page 41) and Bingamens. There are also many walking trails in Kitchener, especially around the Grand River.

Rockway Park has beautifully manicured gardens maintained by the Kitchener Horticultural Society.

Kitchener's City Hall includes a fountain area in the front, which turns into an ice rink for skating in the winter.

Bingemans has a large water park with sides, a wave pool and a splash area. It also has a camping area and golfing.

*Piece of History*

The childhood home of Prime Minister William Lyon Mackenzie King is now the Woodside National Historic Site. It is located in the City of Kitchener. Visitors can tour the home and have a picnic on its beautiful grounds.

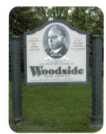

Downtown Kitchener is filled with stores, office buildings, cultural attractions and residences.

The largest performing arts centre in the Region is the Centre In The Square.

# SPECIAL EVENTS

The City of Kitchener coordinates many different special events for its residents. Also, there are many events that are run by Kitchener residents. This makes the City of Kitchener a busy place with a lot for people to do. Check out the table to the right to see some of the festivals and events that occur in the City.

## Some of the Festivals and Special Events in Kitchener

**Hockey Town**: Downtown Kitchener turns into a hub of hockey activities.

**Canada Day**: Includes live music and fireworks in downtown Kitchener.

**KidsSpark**: Has fun activities for children.

**Word on the Street**: A book, reading and magazine festival.

**Winter Holidays**: Many events including a Sanata Claus Parade, the Christkindl Market and light displays.

Classic cars come to downtown Kitchener for the annual Cruising on King event in July.

# UNIQUE QUALITIES
# CITY OF WATERLOO

The City of Waterloo is the smallest of the three cities in Waterloo Region, but it makes a big impact. Waterloo has two universities within its city limits, which is extraordinary for a city of its size. It also has two well-established research institutes, and a sophisticated support system for technology entrepreneurs. Not surprisingly, the City of Waterloo has been named a top intelligent community.[1] Moreover, the City of Waterloo is the city after which Waterloo Region is named.

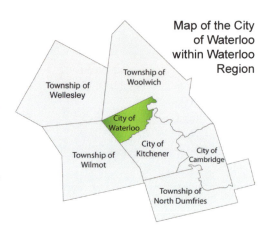

Map of the City of Waterloo within Waterloo Region

Township of Wellesley
Township of Woolwich
City of Waterloo
City of Kitchener
City of Cambridge
Township of Wilmot
Township of North Dumfries

## LAYOUT OF THE CITY

The City of Waterloo's university zone is essentially in the middle of the City, while the downtown area is located in the southern part of Waterloo. The Grand River is located on the east side of Waterloo, while Highway 85 runs north-south in the City. The rest of Waterloo has a varied layout with different areas including residential, commercial and natural areas.

### North Waterloo
North Waterloo has several residential areas including Eastbridge and Colonial Acres. It also has a well-developed business area with many successful companies. The northeastern tip of the City of Waterloo has RIM Park which has exceptional athletic facilities.

### University Area
There are two major universities in the City of Waterloo, University of Waterloo and Wilfrid Laurier University. There are many student residences and apartments in the University Area. Also, there are many local businesses who cater to the university students such as restaurants, sporting good stores, banks and more.

### West
West Waterloo has lovely residential areas. There is also the Laurel Creek Conservation Area.

### South
South Waterloo has the Westmount residential area which has beautiful older homes and large mature trees. In the south, there is also the newer neighborhood of Westvale.

Grey Silo Golf, RIM Park Club
Eastbridge & Colonial Acres
Business Area
Grand River
Lakeshore
Highway 85
Lexington & Lincoln Village
University Downs
Business Area
Laurel Creek Conservation Area
Columbia Lake
University Area
Conestoga College Satalite Campus
Bechtel Park
Erbsville
Laurel Creek Reservoir
Wilfrid Laurier University
Lincoln Heights
University of Waterloo
Waterloo Park
Silver Lake
Uptown
Laurelwood & Columbia Forest
Beachwood
Waterloo Memorial Recreation Complex
Uptown
Clair Hills
Westvale
Westmount
Westmount Golf Club

### East
There are several residential areas and Bechtel Park in the east part of Waterloo. Bechtel Park has a leash free dog park, a forest with trails and soccer fields.

### Uptown Area
Waterloo's downtown area is actually know as Uptown Waterloo. It has a traditional main street with shops and restaurants. There is a mall and a town square in this area. Many company offices are located in Uptown Waterloo. Other interesting places in Uptown Waterloo include: the main branch of the Waterloo Public Library, the Canadian Clay and Glass Gallery, the Perimeter Institute and the Centre for International Governance Innovation.

#### Legend

| | | |
|---|---|---|
| Downtown Area | Golf Course | River or Lake |
| Residential Area | Park or Natural Area | Highway |
| Note: This map is not to scale, it is for general information purposes only. | Business or Industrial Area | |

North
West — East
South

## Quick Facts

People:
- Population of 129,100, this number includes university students;[2]
- 41,530 households;[3]
- Median age is 37.6 years old;[4]
- Primary language spoken at home is English, second is German, third is Chinese.[5]

Land:
- Size of the City is 64.02 kilometers squared;[6]
- Density is 2017 people per kilometer squared;[7]
- The Grand River runs on the east side of the City.

Employment and industry:[8]
- Top three employers in the City are BlackBerry, Manulife Financial, and the University of Waterloo.

Community amenities (excludes the universities' amenities):[9]
- 2 pools and 1 splash pad;
- 3 public library locations;
- 4 indoor arenas and many outdoor ice surfaces;
- Three large parks and many neighborhood parks.

## Name Meaning

The City of Waterloo is named after the Battle of Waterloo that took place in 1815, close to the Town of Waterloo in Belgium. In this Battle, French Emperor Napoleon Bonaparte was defeated by the Seventh Coalition. Part of a painting of the Battle, by William Sadler II, is seen above.

# NOTABLE RESIDENTS

The City of Waterloo has many notable residents, probably the most famous of which is Mike Lazaridis (see page 38) who founded the technology company Research in Motion, later called Blackberry, and the Perimeter Institute. Other notable residents include the City's first mayor Moses Springer and the co-founder of the University of Waterloo, J.G. Hagey.

The first mayor of Waterloo was Moses Springer (1824–1898). He was also one of the Mutual Life Assurance Company's founders and became a Member of Provincial Parliament.

J.G. Hagey (1904–1988) was one of the founders, and the first president, of the University of Waterloo, an institution that has transformed the City. Prior to this, he was the President of Waterloo College (now called Wilfrid Laurier University).

# INTERESTING PLACES

The City of Waterloo has many interesting museums such as the Earth Science Museum, and the Mennonite museum Brubacher House.

The City has several parks including the facilities-rich RIM Park, and the charming Waterloo Park which has an animal farm and a splash pad for children.

Other interesting places include The Canadian Clay and Glass Gallery and the Uptown Waterloo Gallery. The two University campuses are also great places to visit (see pages 32 and 33).

RIM Park has high-quality facilities for the City's residents including: four ice pads, two gymnasiums, a large meeting hall, a golf course, 12 multi-purpose sports fields, 6 baseball diamonds and more.

The Earth Sciences Museum at the University of Waterloo is free and open to the public. Some of its exhibits include dinosaur bones, rocks and several water-related displays.

*Living History*

The above building was once the home of Abraham Erb, one of the first pioneers to settle in Waterloo Region. The building is now the office of a Waterloo law firm.

To the left is the Perimeter Institute for Theoretical Physics. The Institute often has free events for the public.

The Canadian Clay and Glass Gallery is a national museum located in Uptown Waterloo.

# SPECIAL EVENTS

There are many festivals and special events that are held in the City of Waterloo.

Waterloo Town Square has an outdoor area where many of the City's special events are held.

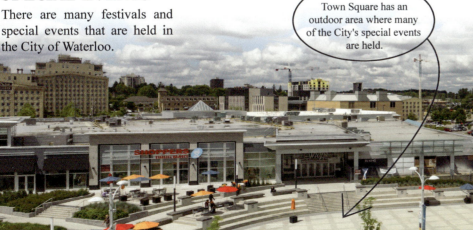

## Some of the Festivals and Events in Waterloo

**Waterloo Buskers Carnival** has street performers from across Canada, and beyond, performing in Uptown Waterloo.

**Canada Day Celebrations** at Columbia Lake in Waterloo includes family-friendly activities and fireworks.

**Royal Medieval Faire** is a festival that recreates a medieval day in Waterloo Park.

**Ice Dogs Festival** (or Winterloo) includes ice sculpture, dog sled rides, skating and food.

# TOWNSHIP OF NORTH DUMFRIES

The Township of North Dumfries has many farms and residential communities. Of all the townships and cities in Waterloo Region, North Dumfries has the smallest population. The Township is full of wonderful natural resources including: fertile soil, small lakes, marshy grasslands and aggregate resources such as sand and gravel.

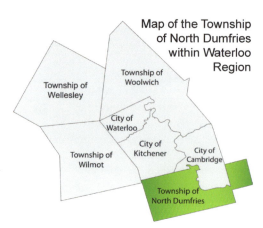

Map of the Township of North Dumfries within Waterloo Region

## LAYOUT OF THE TOWNSHIP

The Township of North Dumfries used be a rectangular shape. However, when the Galt area of the Township was incorporated as a village in 1853, it was "cut out" of the Township, which explains North Dumfries' unusual shape. The Township is known for its roads being set out in a grid-like pattern. The Township is made up of mostly rural areas; however, there are several residential communities in the Township.

### North
In the north part of the Township, you will find the community of Roseville and the historic Detweiler Meetinghouse. Highway 401 is also in this area, as are many farms and an industrial zone.

### Central
The Grand River runs through the central part of the Township. There is also the residential area of Riverview and many farms. Otherwise, most of what used to be the central part of North Dumfries is now the Galt area of the City of Cambridge.

### West
In the west area of North Dumfries, there is the Nith River. The Village of Ayr is in the southwestern part of the Township. Ayr is the largest residential community in North Dumfries.

### East
In the east, you find the residential areas of Branchton, Clyde, Morrison and Clarkson; as well as many farms.

### South
In the south, there are the marshy areas of Wrigely Lake and Bannister Lake. There is also the residential area of Parker and the FWR Dickson Wilderness Area.

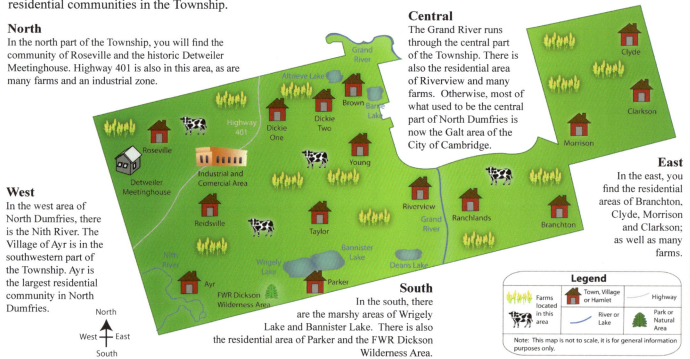

**Legend**

| | | |
|---|---|---|
| Farms located in this area | Town, Village or Hamlet | Highway |
| | River or Lake | Park or Natural Area |

Note: This map is not to scale, it is for general information purposes only.

## Name Meaning

North Dumfries was named after Dumfries, Scotland. Dumfries, Scotland was the hometown of William Dickson (see page 10), who is commonly thought of as the founder of North Dumfries. He bought land in the area of North Dumfries in 1816 and encouraged fellow Scots to settle in the area. To the left is the Midsteeple area of Dumfries, Scotland.

## Quick Facts

People:
- Population of 9,620;[1]
- 3,270 households;[2]
- Median age is 42.1 years old;[3]
- Primary language spoken at home is English, second is Portuguese, third is German.[4]

Land:
- Size of the Township is 187.44 kilometers squared;[5]
- Density is 51 people per kilometer squared;[6]
- The Grand River runs through the middle of the Township.

Employment and industry:[7]
- There are many businesses in the Township including Heritage Transportation Group and Ayr News;
- Agriculture is a significant part of the economy.

Community amenities:[8]
- 2 arenas are maintained by the Township;
- Lawn bowling club and curling club;.
- 11 parks in the Township;
- FWR Dickson Wilderness Area.

## NOTABLE RESIDENTS

There are several notable residents who have lived in North Dumfries Township including: the distinguished botanist John Goldie; Daniel B. Detwelier, a famous promoter of hydropower; and the esteemed physician Ward Woolner (1879–1958) who was president of the Ontario Medical Association and the College of Physicians and Surgeons.

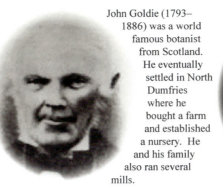

John Goldie (1793–1886) was a world famous botanist from Scotland. He eventually settled in North Dumfries where he bought a farm and established a nursery. He and his family also ran several mills.

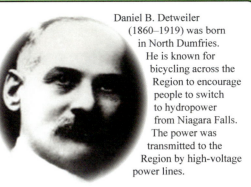

Daniel B. Detweiler (1860–1919) was born in North Dumfries. He is known for bicycling across the Region to encourage people to switch to hydropower from Niagara Falls. The power was transmitted to the Region by high-voltage power lines.

## INTERESTING PLACES

North Dumfries Township has many interesting places. There are heritage buildings such as the Detweiler Meetinghouse; and modern buildings such as the Community Health Centre.

You can enjoy many parks in North Dumfries such as Centennial Park and Victoria Park; as well as natural areas such as the FWR Dickson Wilderness Area.

Driving through the Township can be an enjoyable experience because you can view the rolling hills and farms. It can also be interesting to see an aggregate resource extraction location on your drive.

Centennial Park in the Village of Ayr has a wonderful combination of trees, water, a wooden bridge, and places to sit to enjoy the pretty views.

There are rich aggregate resources in the Township which are mined for construction and other uses.

Living History

The Detweiler Meetinghouse is the oldest Mennonite meetinghouse in Ontario that is made of stone. This Meetinghouse was built in 1855. In 1999, the Detweiler Meetinghouse was restored and is now a place to hold special events.

The Jedburgh creek, mill ponds and dam provide a lovely view. To the left, you can see the area during the cold weather.

The Township has many modern buildings such as the Community Health Centre.

## SPECIAL EVENTS

The largest special event in the Township is the Fresh Ayr Festival which is a family-friendly festival with kids activities, artisans selling their work, and competitions such as Ayr Idol and the Rubber Duck Race.

Other special events have been held in the Township of North Dumfries such as the Ontario Plowing Match which was hosted by the Village of Roseville in 2012.

To the left is a participant in the Ontario Plowing match when it was held in Roseville.

A rubber duck race is sometimes part of the Fresh Ayr Festival.

Driving through North Dumfries Township can be a fun activity because of the lovely views.

# TOWNSHIP OF WELLESLEY

The Township of Wellesley was the last township to be settled in Waterloo Region. The Township has many farms and several villages; as well as two rivers and many forests. Interestingly, compared to the Region's other cities and townships, the Township of Wellesley's population is the youngest, with a median age of 32.3 years.[1]

Map of the Township of Wellesley within Waterloo Region

Township of Wellesley
Township of Woolwich
City of Waterloo
City of Kitchener
City of Cambridge
Township of Wilmot
Township of North Dumfries

## LAYOUT OF THE TOWNSHIP

The Township of Wellesley is composed of mostly agricultural land. There are several villages in the Township which are mostly located in the southern and eastern parts of the Township. Regional Highway 86 runs along the northeastern border of the Township. There is the Conestoga River on the east side of the Township, and the Nith River in the southwestern part of the Township.

### West
The western area of Wellesley Township is primarily composed of farms. There are also several sections of forest.

### Central
This area includes the community of Crosshill which has the Region's oldest township office building. There are many farms in this area.

### North
The northern area has many farms. There is also Regional Road 86 which leads to the City of Waterloo going east and towards Lake Huron going west. Part of the Conestoga River is located in the northeastern part of the Township.

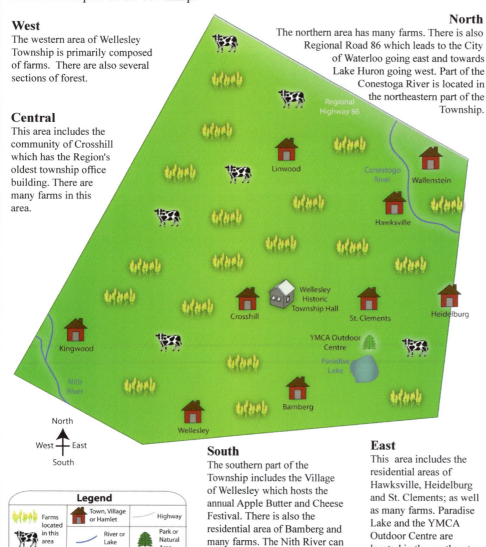

Regional Highway 86
Linwood
Conestoga River
Wallenstein
Hawksville
Wellesley Historic Township Hall
Crosshill
St. Clements
Heidelburg
Kingwood
YMCA Outdoor Centre
Paradise Lake
Nith River
Bamberg
Wellesley

North
West — East
South

### Legend
Farms located in this area
Town, Village or Hamlet
Highway
River or Lake
Park or Natural Area

Note: This map is not to scale, it is for general information purposes only.

### South
The southern part of the Township includes the Village of Wellesley which hosts the annual Apple Butter and Cheese Festival. There is also the residential area of Bamberg and many farms. The Nith River can be found in the southwestern part of Wellesley.

### East
This area includes the residential areas of Hawksville, Heidelburg and St. Clements; as well as many farms. Paradise Lake and the YMCA Outdoor Centre are located in the southeastern part of the Township.

## Quick Facts

People:
- Population of 10,920;[2]
- 3,200 households;[3]
- Median age is 32.3 years old;[4]
- Primary language spoken at home is English, second is German, third is Dutch.[5]

Land:
- Size of the Township is 277.79 kilometers squared;[6]
- Density is 39.31 people per kilometer squared;[7]
- The Conestoga River runs on the east side of the city.

Employment and industry:[8]
- Top employers are Jones Feed Mill and EMB Manufacturing, as well as work in agriculture.

Community amenities:[9]
- 4 community centres, 2 of which have arenas;
- Several baseball diamonds and soccer fields;
- 3 public library branches.

### Name Meaning

The Township was originally called the "Queen's Bush" because the Township's lands were set aside to provide for the Protestant Church. However, it was later named Wellesley Township after the British Statesman Lord Richard Colley Wellesley (1760–1842), pictured above. Lord Wellesley worked as a British administrator in India and, later, Ireland.

# NOTABLE RESIDENTS

Wellesley Township has many notable residents. For example, Governor General David Johnson lived in the Township for several years while he was president of the University of Waterloo.

Dr. Debrah Glaister is a famous doctor from Wellesley Township. Another esteemed former resident of the Township is horseshoe pitching champion, Elmer Hohl (1919–1987).

Dr. Debrah Glaister (1906–1985) was born in Wellesley Township. She was the Township's first female physician. She also worked as a doctor in the Royal Canadian Army in 1943. She eventually became Chief of Staff of Kitchener's Freeport Hospital.

David Johnston (born 1945) was the President of the University of Waterloo from 1999 to 2010. He was appointed as the Governor General of Canada in 2010. He is Canada's 28th governor general.

# INTERESTING PLACES

There are many beautiful historic buildings in Wellesley Township, several of which are still in use such as the Wellesley Township Hall and St. John's Evangelical Lutheran Church.

The Township is a treat to drive through with its views of rolling hills, farms and forests. In addition, the YMCA runs an outdoor centre located on the shores of the lovely Paradise Lake.

St. John's Evangelical Lutheran Church was built from wood in 1852. A new church was built in 1872, after the wood church burnt down. This church is still used about four times each year.

## Living History

The Wellesley Township Hall, above, was built in 1855. It is still used as the Wellesley Township Council Chamber.

This historic school was built in the Village of Wellesley in 1898. It now houses the Wellesley Historical Society and the Wellesly Branch of the Region of Waterloo Library.

The YMCA Outdoor Centre and Camp Ki-Wa-Y are located on Paradise Lake in Wellesley Township. A wide variety of great outdoor activities are offered for both registered groups and campers.

The countryside in Wellesley Township provides spectacular views with a beautiful variety of fields and forests.

# SPECIAL EVENTS

There are several festivals that are held in the Township. The Wellesley Apple Butter and Cheese Festival is held in the Village of Wellesley and includes good food and family-friendly activities. There is also the annual Fall Fair which includes a parade in the Village of Wellesley, as well as the sale of fall foods and more.

Good food is a hallmark of the Apple Butter and Cheese Festival held in Wellesley each September.

To the right is an image from the Wellesley Fall Fair Parade.

# UNIQUE QUALITIES

# TOWNSHIP OF WILMOT

The Township of Wilmot has a great mix of rural and urban areas. Wilmot Township is well known for several of its special events such as the Mennonite Relief Sale. Of all the townships, Wilmot is the most densely populated with 76 people per square kilometer.[1]

Map of the Township of Wilmot within Waterloo Region

## LAYOUT OF THE TOWNSHIP

Wilmot Township has Highway 7/8 which crosses Wilmot in an east–west direction. Highway 7/8 allows for an easy drive across the Township to the towns of New Hamburg and Baden. The Nith River runs in a north–south direction in the Township. There is Lake Adler in the south of the Township, and Sunfish Lake in the north. Many farms are located throughout Wilmot Township.

### North
The north part of Wilmot includes the communities of St. Agatha and Lisbon. You can also find the charming Sunfish Lake and part of the Nith River in the north. Most of the land in this area is used for agricultural purposes.

### Central
In the middle of the Township, you can find the Oasis in the Centre park. There is also the Town of Baden and the community of Foxboro Green. Highway 7/8 also runs through the middle of the Township.

### East
In the east area of Wilmot Township, there are many farms. The communities of Petersburg and Mannheim are located in the east part of the Township as well. There is the Dundee Country Club in the southeastern part of the Township.

### West
This area includes the Township's biggest town, New Hamburg, which has a population of 11,953 people.[10] The Nith river is also on the west side of the Township.

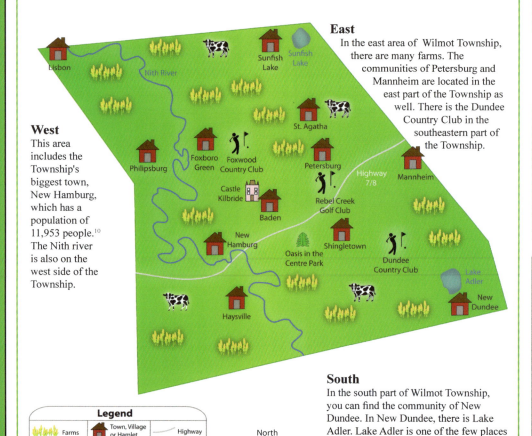

### South
In the south part of Wilmot Township, you can find the community of New Dundee. In New Dundee, there is Lake Adler. Lake Adler is one of the few places in the Region where lakeside living is possible. There is also the community of Haysville in the south, as well as several farms.

**Legend** — Farms located in this area; Town, Village or Hamlet; Highway; River or Lake; Park or Natural Area. Note: This map is not to scale, it is for general information purposes only.

North West East South

## Quick Facts

People:
- Population of 20,110;[2]
- 7,200 households;[3]
- Median age is 40.4 years old;[4]
- Primary language spoken at home is English, second is German, third is Dutch.[5]

Land:
- Size of the Township is 263.72 squared kilometers;[6]
- Density of 76 people per squared kilometer;[7]
- The Nith River runs on the west side of the Township;
- Highway 7/8 runs through the Township.

Employment and industry:[8]
- Top employers include Erb Transportation, Waterloo Region District School Board, and Ontario Drive and Gear.

Community amenities:[9]
- Wilmot Recreation Complex which has two arenas and a swimming pool;
- New Hamburg Complex which has an arena and a community centre;
- 4 more community centres;
- Approximately 193 acres of parkland.

## Name Meaning

Wilmot Township was named after Sir Robert John Wilmot-Horton (1784–1841), pictured above. He was known for being Under-Secretary of State for War and the Colonies and for his writing promoting emigration to the colonies.

60

## NOTABLE RESIDENTS

Many famous people have lived in Wilmot Township. For example, Sir Adam Beck, the founder of Ontario Power Generation (HydroOne) lived in the Township. Elsie Cressman, a leader in midwifery, also lived in Wilmot Township. Another notable resident was Laverne Roth (1901–1978) who was born in Wilmot Township, and spent 10 years playing hockey in the National Hockey League.

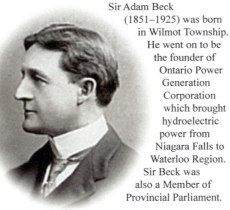

Sir Adam Beck (1851–1925) was born in Wilmot Township. He went on to be the founder of Ontario Power Generation Corporation which brought hydroelectric power from Niagara Falls to Waterloo Region. Sir Beck was also a Member of Provincial Parliament.

Elsie Cressman (1923–2012) was a Wilmot resident and a midwife. She helped establish medical clinics in Africa and promoted the profession of midwifery in Canada.

## INTERESTING PLACES

There are many interesting places in Wilmot Township including the National Historic Site, Castle Kilbride; New Hamburg's charming downtown (see page 22); the Oasis in the Centre Park; Sunfish Lake; and several golf clubs including Rebel Creek Golf Club and the Dundee Country Club.

Photo by Lynn B.

The largest water wheel in North America is found in New Hamburg. The Heritage Water Wheel is 50 feet high. It is located on the Nith River in Scott Park. The wheel was built in 1990.

Living History

Castle Kilbride is located in Baden. It was built by James Livingston in 1877. Mr. Livingston made his fortune growing flax and producing linseed oil. The Wilmot Township offices are built behind this Castle, integrating the two sites.

The Oasis in the Centre is a park that was built in the year 2000 to celebrate Wilmot Township's 150th anniversary.

Sunfish Lake is located in the north part of Wilmot. There are restrictions on the use of Sunfish Lake to keep it healthy.

Baden Hills

The Baden Hills have the highest elevation in the Region.

## SPECIAL EVENTS

There are many special events held in Wilmot Township. The largest event is the Mennonite Relief Sale which raises money for charity. Another popular event is the Strawberry Festival held in St. Agatha each year. Other festivals that are held in the Township include: New Hamburg Live which celebrates the arts; Moparfest which celebrates the Mopar Car; and the New Hamburg Fall Fair.

St. Agatha has an annual Strawberry festival every year in June. The festival includes lots of delicious food and family-friendly activities.

The Mennonite Relief Sale is the largest event in Wilmot Township. Quilts, food and plants are sold to raise money to help those experiencing poverty around the world. The sale brings in over 30,000 visitors every year.

# TOWNSHIP OF WOOLWICH

The Township of Woolwich has the largest population of Waterloo Region's four townships. The Township is home to the Region of Waterloo International Airport, the St. Jacobs Farmers' Market and three golf courses. There are also many farms and residential communities in Woolwich.

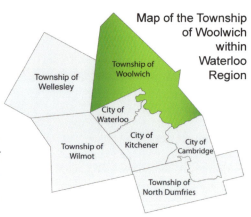

Map of the Township of Woolwich within Waterloo Region

## LAYOUT OF THE TOWNSHIP

The Township of Woolwich has the Conestogo River on the west side of the Township and the Grand River on the east side. Most of the land in the Township is used for agriculture. There are several residential communities including St. Jacobs, Elmira and Breslau. Regional Highway 85 goes through part of the Township.

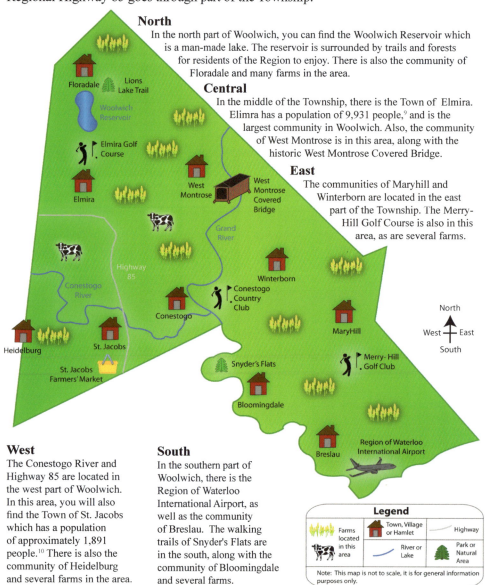

**North**
In the north part of Woolwich, you can find the Woolwich Reservoir which is a man-made lake. The reservoir is surrounded by trails and forests for residents of the Region to enjoy. There is also the community of Floradale and many farms in the area.

**Central**
In the middle of the Township, there is the Town of Elmira. Elimra has a population of 9,931 people,[9] and is the largest community in Woolwich. Also, the community of West Montrose is in this area, along with the historic West Montrose Covered Bridge.

**East**
The communities of Maryhill and Winterborn are located in the east part of the Township. The Merry-Hill Golf Course is also in this area, as are several farms.

**West**
The Conestogo River and Highway 85 are located in the west part of Woolwich. In this area, you will also find the Town of St. Jacobs which has a population of approximately 1,891 people.[10] There is also the community of Heidelburg and several farms in the area.

**South**
In the southern part of Woolwich, there is the Region of Waterloo International Airport, as well as the community of Breslau. The walking trails of Snyder's Flats are in the south, along with the community of Bloomingdale and several farms.

### Legend
| | | |
|---|---|---|
| Farms located in this area | Town, Village or Hamlet | Highway |
| | River or Lake | Park or Natural Area |

Note: This map is not to scale, it is for general information purposes only.

## Quick Facts

People:
- Population of 24,400;[1]
- 8,270 households;[2]
- Median age is 38.6 years old;[3]
- Primary language spoken at home is English, second is German, third is Dutch.[4]

Land:
- Size of the Township 326.17 kilometers squared;[5]
- Density is 75 people per kilometers squared;[6]
- Conestogo River and Grand River run through the Township.

Employment and industry:[7]
- Top employers include Home Hardware, Trim Masters and Walmart;
- Region of Waterloo International Airport is located in the Township.

Community amenities:[8]
- The Woolwich Memorial Centre is a sports facility with 2 large ice surfaces and a public pool;
- 80 kilometers of trails;
- 4 community centres and 3 community halls.

## Name Meaning

Woolwich Township was named after a town in England named Woolwich, which was part the county of Kent, but is now part of greater London. Above is a picture of the Woolwich Royal Aresnal Gatehouse in Woolwich, England.

# NOTABLE RESIDENTS

Many of Woolwich Township's residents have become well known. For example, Home Hardware founder Walter Hachborn (born 1921) is from Woolwich. Best-selling nonfiction writer Malcolm Gladwell (see page 47) grew up in the Township. Also, the long-time leader of the Municipality of Waterloo Region, Ken Seiling, is from the Township; as is hockey great Darryl Sittler.

Ken Seiling, a Woolwich resident, was the Woolwich Township Mayor for seven years. He has been elected as Regional Chair for Waterloo Region nine times. Mr. Seiling was also the founding Director of the Wellington County Museum and Archives.

Darryl Sittler (born 1950) was raised in St. Jacobs. He played in the National Hockey League starting in 1970, including 15 years with the Toronto Maple Leafs. On the left, Darryl is signing autographs at the Kitchener Memorial Auditorium.

# INTERESTING PLACES

Woolwich Township is full of interesting places to discover. For example, in the Town of St. Jacobs there is a lovely farmers' market, a charming downtown, and several theatres and museums.

In Woolwich Township, there are both historic structures such as the West Montrose Covered Bridge; and modern buildings such as the Woolwich Memorial Centre. Moreover, there are many walking trails and golf courses.

In the Township's countryside, you will often see Old Order Mennonite farmers still using horses to travel.

## Living History

The West Montrose Covered Bridge, often referred to as the "Kissing Bridge," is a covered bridge found in the community of West Montrose. It is the only remaining covered bridge in Ontario. The bridge was built in 1881 and is 198 feet in length.

Woolwich Memorial Centre is a modern sporting facility with ice rinks and a pool.

The St. Jacobs Farmers' Market is a popular market that is open all year. It has food vendors as well as artisans and more.

If you take a drive on the country roads in Woolwich Township you can still see Old Order Mennonites using horse-drawn buggies, similar to the one above.

The Merry-Hill Golf Course, seen to the left, is one of three enjoyable golf courses located in Woolwich Township.

# SPECIAL EVENTS

The Township of Woolwich hosts the "world's largest one day maple syrup festival," the Elmira Maple Syrup Festival.[1]

There are many other events held in Woolwich Township including: the Kissing Bridge Artists Studio Tour, the Elmira Charity Quilt Auction and Country Market, and the Summer Concert Series held in Elmira's Gore Park. A leisurely drive through this lovely Township can also feel like a special occasion.

The Elmira Maple Syrup Festival features delicious foods that are covered with maple syrup such as pancakes; as well as many other tasty treats. There are family-friendly activities and the opportunity to tour a farm to see how maple syrup is retrieved from maple trees and boiled to make syrup.

## REGIONAL GLUE
# NEIGHBOURS WORKING TOGETHER

One reason why Waterloo Region feels like a cohesive community is that the vast majority of people who live in Waterloo Region also work in Waterloo Region.

## REGIONAL BUSINESSES AND BUSINESS ORGANIZATIONS

Waterloo Region residents work together within local businesses, social-profit organizations, community organizations and local governments. In fact, approximately eighty percent of the Region's residents who are employed, work in Waterloo Region.[1]

Members of the community work together to promote the Region across Canada, and the world; with the goal of bringing investment and talented employees to Waterloo Region. In fact, there are organizations for whom promoting Waterloo Region is part of their mandate, such as Canada's Technology Triangle.

The median commuting distance to work in Waterloo Region is 5.8 km, which is well below the Ontario average.[2]

Organizations such as Canada's Technology Triangle and Communitech work to promote Waterloo Region as an ideal place to invest, work and start new businesses. These efforts help keep the local economy and jobs flourishing.

There are many business organizations in the Region that allow people to network and build working relationships including: the Kitchener-Waterloo Chamber of Commerce, the Cambridge Chamber of Commerce, New Hamburg Board of Trade, and the Small Business Community Network.

### Piece of History

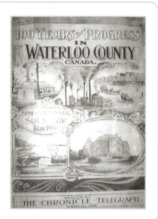

Residents of the Region celebrated their progress in the booklet: *100 Years of Progress in Waterloo County Canada*. The publication outlined the Region's successes from 1806 to 1906. It also included information on important local industries like agriculture, insurance and manufacturing. Prominent local residents, and their homes, were featured as well. Even then, the community worked together and celebrated the progress it made together.

Approximately

# 80%

of working people who live in Waterloo Region, work in Waterloo Region.[3]

The residents of Waterloo Region work together to create approximately 30 billion dollars of gross domestic product.[4] Regional businesses export billions of dollars of goods and services.

# REGIONAL GOVERNMENT

While each city and township in Waterloo Region has an elected mayor and council to make decisions for their specific area, there is also a municipal level of government which serves all three cities and four townships. The Regional Government for Waterloo Region is made up of the Regional Chair, eight directly-elected councillors, and the mayors of each township and city. Regional Government in Waterloo Region works to create a thriving and balanced Region. The Regional Government's responsibilities include creating a plan for how the Region should grow, as well as providing a wide range of services for residents of the Region.

> " ... an inclusive, thriving and sustainable community committed to maintaining harmony between rural and urban areas and fostering opportunities for current and future generations. "
>
> — Region of Waterloo Municipal Government's vision statement[1]

Maintaining a healthy balance between urban and rural areas of Waterloo Region is a crucial job of Regional Government.

 Taking care of drinking water and treating waste water are important Regional services.

 Public health initiatives are part of Regional Government services.

The first ever Blue Box recycling program was tested in Waterloo Region in 1983. The program asks residents to put their recyclable waste materials in a Blue Box beside their garbage on their garbage pick-up day. The recyclables are then collected and sent to recycling facilities. Similar Blue Box programs can now be found across Canada.

## More Region of Waterloo Municipal Government Services [2]

- Garbage collection and waste management.
- Public transit including Grand River Transit.
- Construction and maintenance of regional roads.

- Implementing income assistance programs.
- Providing employment programs.
- Overseeing several childcare and infant development programs.
- Emergency preparedness planning.

The Region of Waterloo funds many cultural endeavors that help preserve the Region's shared and diverse heritage. The Waterloo Region Museum, pictured below, has almost 50,000 historical artifacts related to the Region in its collection.[3] The museum also includes a 60 acre living history museum called Doon Heritage Village which demonstrates how people lived in 1914.[4]

# NEIGHBOURS HELPING NEIGHBOURS

Waterloo Region has a rich history of community building and helping people in need. There are many charities and not-for-profit organizations run by residents in Waterloo Region.

There are several organizations in the Region that help people who need shelter such as Women's Crisis Services and Heartwood Place.

## REGIONAL CHARITIES AND NOT-FOR-PROFIT ORGANIZATIONS

Waterloo Region has a vibrant not-for-profit and charitable sector with many dedicated staff and volunteers who work hard to make the Region a better place. Some examples of effective not-for-profit organizations include: The Food Bank of Waterloo Region which distributes food to those in need; Hospice of Waterloo Region which helps support those who are very ill; and Strong Start which helps children learn to read.

Hospice of Waterloo Region is just one of many organizations that work to help people who are ill in Waterloo Region.

The Kitchener and Waterloo Community Foundation sponsors a Random Act of Kindness Day which promotes acts of kindness in the Region.

The Food Bank of Waterloo Region coordinates the collection and distribution of food to help people who have a hard time making ends meet.

There are several organizations that try to cultivate and support local volunteer leaders such as Leadership Waterloo Region and Capacity Waterloo Region.

Regional environmental groups include Community CarShare which helps people share a car to reduce pollution and save money; and Sustainable Waterloo Region which helps people reduce their organizations' carbon footprint.

There are many ways that people in Waterloo Region come together to help children. Nutrition for Learning provides children with free food to help them focus on school, not on being hungry. While Strong Start helps students learn to read.

### Piece of History

A "barnraising" is when the Mennonite community gathers together to rebuild a neighbour's barn. Because so many people help, the barn is built in one day. It is a Mennonite tradition that often takes place in Waterloo Region. It is the perfect example of neighbours helping neighbours. To the left is an image of a 1968 barnraising in Waterloo.

# NEIGHBOURS CELEBRATING TOGETHER

There are many ways that people in Waterloo Region celebrate together including participating in festivals, honouring people with awards, and taking part in many other events.

## REGIONAL CELEBRATIONS AND AWARDS

Waterloo Region has many events where residents can come together and have fun throughout the year. Some of the biggest festivals include the Elmira Maple Syrup Festival and the Kitchener-Waterloo Oktoberfest Festival.

Regional residents have the opportunity to show their appreciation to people who have made a special contribution to Waterloo Region through several awards such as induction into the Waterloo Region Hall of Fame.

The biggest festival in the Region is the Kitchener-Waterloo Oktoberfest Festival. No longer just held in the City of Kitchener, there are Festhallen all across the Region. Also, the Oktoberfest Parade is the biggest parade in the Region.

The Waterloo Region Hall of Fame is a way that community residents celebrate exceptional citizens who have notably contributed to the community or demonstrated exceptional achievement in their professional endeavors.

The *Waterloo Region Record* is the Region's largest newspaper. It sponsors two important awards. The "Top 40 under 40 award" celebrates 40 exceptional young people in the Region who have excelled and are under 40 years of age, while the *Waterloo Region Record's* "Barnraiser Award" is an award that recognizes an individual who works with others towards the betterment of the Waterloo Region community.

There are free Canada Day celebrations across the Waterloo Region.

There are several Santa Claus parades, Christmas light displays, and special Christmas markets in the Region during the winter holidays.

### Piece of History

Saengerfest was a music festival celebrated in the Region in 1875, 1879 and 1886. It was a spectacle of music and dancing that featured choirs from many cities including Detriot, Chicago and Montreal. Saengerfest also celebrated German heritage and music. The festival was reported on across Canada. To the left is a picture of people gathered together for one of the Saengerfest celebrations that occurred between 1875–1886.

# JUST A DRIVE

There are many great places that are just a drive away from Waterloo Region. Whether you are looking for the excitement of Canada's largest city or a quiet trip to the beach, it can be just an hour or two to get there by car.

The City of Toronto is just an hour and ten minutes by car from Waterloo Region. Toronto is Canada's largest city and offers a plethora of amenities including many restaurants, museums, theatres and stores. There are also large attractions such as the CN Tower, professional sports teams and the Ontario Science Centre.

The Toronto Zoo celebrates animals from all over the world and is about an hour and fifteen minutes away by car. While the African Lion Safari recreates a safari experience and is just minutes away from the City of Cambridge.

You can find terrific skiing and snowboarding at Blue Mountain Resort in Grey County, which is just a two hour drive north of the Region.

The Stratford Festival is a classical theatre festival that runs from April to October, in Stratford, Ontario. The City of Stratford is about a 30 minute drive from the Region. The festival has world-class theatre productions. To the right is Seana McKenna as Elizabeth, from the Stratford production of Mary Stuart.

Lake Huron and its lovely beaches are about an hour and half drive from Waterloo Region.

# BRIGHT FUTURE

Waterloo Region has a bright future for many reasons. First, the Region is filled with talented, skilled and creative people that help build the community and its economy. Second, the Region's local universities and institutes help create new, cutting-edge research and innovation; and entrepreneurs are encouraged to use these innovations to create new companies. And finally, Waterloo Region's residents work to preserve the Region's heritage and environment, making Waterloo Region a great place with a bright future.

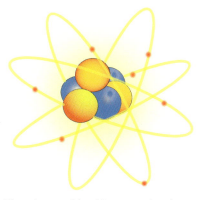

There is ground-breaking research going on in Waterloo Region at local universities, think tanks and technology companies.

Waterloo Region is particularly good at mixing the old and new. To the left is a good example, with the Waterloo Heritage Train in the foreground and new modern apartments being built in the background. This picture is from the City of Waterloo.

Entrepreneurship, innovation, and taking on business challenges are qualities that are celebrated in Waterloo Region

Waterloo Region has great educational opportunities that help people grow and develop a broad range of valuable skills.

Great ideas are developed in the Region with smart, creative people working together.

Local government officials, environmental organizations, and residents work hard to protect the environment for the future generations.

# FINDING OUT MORE
# RESOURCES

## Local Government

**Region of Waterloo**
Phone: 519-575-4400
www.regionofwaterloo.ca

**City of Waterloo**
Phone: 519-886-1550
www.waterloo.ca

**City of Cambridge**
Phone: 519-623-1340
www.cambridge.ca

**Township of Woolwich**
Phone: 519-669-1647
www.woolwich.ca

**City of Kitchener**
Phone: 519-741-2345
www.kitchener.ca

**Township of Wellesley**
Phone: 519-699-4611
www.township.wellesley.on.ca

**Township of Wilmot**
Phone: 519-634-8444
www.wilmot.ca

**Township of North Dumfries**
Phone: 519-621-0340
www.northdumfries.ca

## Education

**University of Waterloo**
Phone: 519-888-4567
www.uwaterloo.ca

**Wilfrid Laurier University**
Phone: 519-884-1970
www.wlu.ca

**Waterloo District Public School Board**
Phone: 519-570-0003
www.wrdsb.ca

**Waterloo Catholic District School Board**
Phone: 519-578-3660
www.wcdsb.ca

**Conestoga College**
Phone: 519-748-5220
www.conestogac.on.ca

**French Language School Boards**
www.csdccs.edu.on.ca
www.csviamonde.ca/csviamonde/index.php

### Private Grade Schools
- Fellowship Christian School, www. kwfcs.com
- Foundation Christian School, www.onarock.ca
- K-W Montessori School, www.kwmontessorischool.com
- Kitchener-Waterloo Bilingual School, www.kwbilingualschool.com
- St. Judes School, www.stjudes.com
- Scholars' Hall, www.scholarshall.com
- Laurentian Hills Christian School, www.lhcs.ws
- Rockway Mennonite Collegiate, www.rockway.ca
- St. John's-Kilmarnock School, www.sjkschool.org

### Private Career Colleges
- Liason College, www.liaisonkitchener.ca
- Trios College, www.trios.com
- Gina's College, www.ginascollege.com
- Medix College, www.medixcollege.ca

## Business Development

**Communtiech**
Phone: 519-888-9944
www.communitech.ca

**Accelerator Centre**
Phone: 519-342-2400
www.acceleratorcentre.com

**Canada's Technology Triangle**
Phone: 519-747-2541
www.techtriangle.com

**Canadian Innovation Centre**
Phone: 519-885-5870
www.innovationcentre.ca

**Greater Kitchener-Waterloo Chamber of Commerce**
Phone: 519-576-5000
www.greaterkwchamber.com

**Cambridge Chamber of Commerce**
Phone: 519-622-2221
www.cambridgechamber.com

**Waterloo Region Small Business Centres**
Phone: 519-741-2604
www.waterlooregionsmallbusiness.com

### More Business Organizations:
- New Hamburg Board of Trade, www.nhbot.ca
- Baden and District Chamber of Commerce, www.wilmot.ca/badenchamber
- Small Business Community Network, www.sbcncanada.org
- Downtown Kitchener BIA, www.kitchenerdowntown.com
- Uptown Waterloo BIA, www.uptownwaterloobia.com
- Galt on the Grand, Downtown Cambridge BIA, www.galtonthegrand.ca

## Events & Hospitality

**Explore Waterloo Region**
www.explorewaterlooregion.com
This is the Region's official tourism site with information on places to stay and things to do in the Region.

**SNAPD KW**
www.snapkw.com
The SNAPD website has a great community calendar.

**Grand Social**
www.grandsocial.ca
This website highlights community arts and culture events.

**Waterloo Sports Express**
www.waterloosportsxpress.ca
Local sports events and results are listed on this website.

**KW Kids**
www.kwkids.com
There is a listing of community events for kids and families.

**KW Oktoberfest**
www.oktoberfest.ca
This is the website for the Waterloo Region's largest festival.

**Waterloo Region Record**
www.therecord.com
The Region's largest newspaper has an extensive online listing of community events.

# Details

## *Images*

Pg. 1: Cityscape courtesy Matthew Smith.
Pgs. 2 and 3: Farm by JMO.
Pg. 4: Map of Canada, Outline by Lokal_Profil modified by Paul Robinson accessed at http://commons.wikimedia.org/wiki/File:Canada_blank_map.svg, then modified by JMO (CC) | Map of Waterloo Region within Southern Ontario, modified from: Southern Ontario, St. Catharines, Ontario: Brock University Map Library. Available: Brock University Map Library Controlled Access http://www.brocku.ca/maplibrary/maps/outline/Ontario/sont.jpg | Clock accessed from http://pixabay.com/en/time-clock-watch-46327/ | Map of Waterloo Region by JMO base Regional of Waterloo municipal maps (hereafter WR-map).
Pg. 5: Population increase by alexmillos/Shutterstock.com | Grand River by Chris Hill/Shutterstock.com | Farm by JMO | Gravel accessed from http://pixabay.com/en/gravel-rock-stones-grey-20903 | Rolling Hills accessed at http://vitacollections.ca/kpl-gsr/details.asp?ID=47030, Waterloo Historical Society Collection | Forest by JMO.
Pg. 6: Arrow and Banner Stones courtesy of the Museum of Ontario Archaeology | Pottery by JMO on Rare Research Reserve archaeology walk | Longhouse by SF photo/Shutterstock.com | Huron Natural Area by JMO.
Pg. 7: Joseph Brant by James Boswell c. 1776, Library Archives Canada, ACC 1970-188-2367 | Sir Frederick Haldimand (1718-1791) by John Francis Rigaud accessed at http://commons.wikimedia.org/wiki/File:Sir_Frédéric_Haldimand_IMG_3174.JPG | Thomas Ridout map, Public Archives of Canada, accessed on wikipedia at http://commons.wikimedia.org/wiki/File:Thomas_Ridout_map_of_Grand_River_Indian_Lands,_1821.jpg | Painting by Elizabeth Simcoe, 1793.
Pg. 8: Pensylvannia in North America, modified by JMO of Map of North America, by Alex Covarrubia, accessed at http://commons.wikimedia.org/wiki/File:North_America_second_level_political_division_2.svg (CC) | Covered Wagon by Nancy Hochmuth/Shutterstock.com | Horses by Conny Sjostrom/Shutterstock.com | Clear Forest/Crib/House all courtesy Joseph Schneider Haus.
Pg. 9: Fraktur courtesy Joseph Schneider Haus | Mennonite Meeting House by Hunsberger Photograpy courtesy Mennonite Archives of Ontario | Quilting by Hunsberger Photography courtesy Mennonite Archives of Ontario | Pioneer Settlers Memorial Tower courtesy of City of Kitchener Photo Galleries | Mennonite Story by JMO.
Pg. 10: Map of United Kingdom within Europe/and Scotland within United Kingdom adjusted by JMO of Location European nation states by Ssolbergj accessed at http://en.wikipedia.org/wiki/File:Location_European_nation_states.svg [Europe map by Ssolberi from wikipedia hereafter Europe_Ssolberi_wikipedia] (CC) | Bagpiper by Anneka/Shutterstock.com | William Dickson courtesy City of Cambridge Archives | Sailing Ship ca.1840, Peter Winkworth, Collection of Canadiana, Artist unknown | Peter Jaffray courtesy Waterloo Region Hall of Fame | McDougall Cottage by JMO.
Pg. 11: England/Ireland within United Kingdom adjusted by JMO map of Europe_Ssolberi_wikipedia (CC) | Queen Victoria Statue by JMO | British immigrant children, Isaac Erb/Library and Archives Canada/PA-04785 | Frederick Hobson accessed at http://upload.wikimedia.org/wikipedia/commons/f/fa/Frederick_Hobson.jpg | Thomas Hilard courtesy Waterloo Region Hall of Fame | Emigrants leaving Ireland by Henry Doyle (1886) accessed at http://en.wikipedia.org/wiki/File:Emigrants_Leave_Ireland_by_Henry_Doyle_1868.jpg | Leprechaun by Pushkin/Shutterstock.com.
Pg. 12: Germany within Europe adjusted Location European nation states by Europe_Ssolberi_wikipedia (CC) | Jacob Hailer courtesy Waterloo Region Hall of Fame | Emil Vogelsang courtesy Waterloo Region Hall of Fame | Lang Tannery, University of Waterloo Library, Lang Tanning Fonds, Belair Photo.
Pg. 13: Concordia Club courtesy Concordia Club | German Flag from wikipedia accessed at http://en.wikipedia.org/wiki/File:Flag_of_Germany.svg | Christmas tree by Tischenko Irina/Shutterstock.com. | Onkle Hans courtesy of KW Oktoberfest | Schnitzel by Simone Voigt/Shutterstock.com | Beer by Nitr/Shutterstock.com | Drindle from PRILL/Shutterstock.com.
Pg 14: Map of NewFoundland in North American modified from North America Blank Range Map by Alan Rockefeller accessed at http://commons.wikimedia.org/wiki/File:North_america_blank_range_map.png (CC) | Woman working at textile mill courtesy of the Kitchener Public Library, from Toronto Star | Bell Island by V. J. Matthew/Shutterstock.com | Officer and His Bride, Canada Dept. of National Defence/Library and Archives Canada/PA-008179.
Pg. 15: Portugal within Europe adjusted by JMO from Europe_Ssolberi_wikipedia (CC) | Manuael Cabral courtesy City of Cambridge Archives | Monument by JMO | Luis de Camoens by Fernão Gomes accessed at http://en.wikipedia.org/wiki/File:Camões,_por_Fernão_Gomes.jpg | Flag of Portugal (PD) accessed from wikipedia at http://en.wikipedia.org/wiki/File:Flag_of_Portugal.svg | Pier 21 by EPG_EuroPhotoGraphics/Shutterstock.com.
Pg. 16: Four person family by Goodluz/Shutterstock.com | Norman Lynn by David McCammon courtesy Waterloo Region Hall of Fame | Multicultural Festival by JMO | Two person family by Flashon Studio/Shutterstock.com.
Pg. 17: Two person couple by Rob/Fotolia.com | Three person family by Carlos Santa Maria /Fotolia.com | Wedding Bands by VERSUSstudio/Shutterstock.com | Couple with heart from Pixabay.com |Part of Shantz Family Reunion by Denton Photography Studio accessed at http://www3.sympatico.ca/darrenarndt/shantz/1930shantz-photo2.htm.
Pg. 18: Large home – the Kim Family Home built in Waterloo by George Milla Construction Limited | Townhomes Courtesy of City of Cambridge Photo Gallery | Condo Residence courtesy of City of Kitchener Photo Gallery | Retirement Home courtesy of City of Cambridge Photo Gallery | Older Homes courtesy of City of Cambridge Photo Galleries | Joseph Schnieder Haus courtesy of City of Kitchener Photo Galleries.
Pg 19: Magazine courtesy Buy Sell Improve – Homes Plus | Realtor by Rob/Fotolia.com | The Bauer Lofts courtesy City of Waterloo Photo Galleries.
Pg. 20: Bicyclist by Steamroller/Fotolia.com | School Bus by Dzain/Fotolia.com | Hybrid Bus courtesy Grand River Transit | Horse Drawn Street Car from Waterloo Public Library collection.
Pg. 21: Highway courtesy Scott Steeves | Classic Train by JMO | Airplane by MO:SES/Fotolia.com | Via Rail Train accessed from http://en.wikipedia.org/wiki/File:LRC_Club_Car.jpg | Midnight Sun Car courtesy Midnight Sun Solar Race Car Team | Horse & Buggy by razvanmatei /Fotolia.com.
Pg. 22: Market vegetables Baloncici/Shutterstock.com | Fashion shopping by michaeljung/Shutterstock.com | Downtown New Hamburg image by JMO | Sale Bag by Vectomart/Shutterstock.com | Shopping online by Goodluz/Shutterstock.com | Hollinger & Home Hardware images courtesy of Home Hardware.
Pg. 23: Aquarium by ET1972/Shutterstock | Kitten by Tony Campbell /Fotolia.com | Puppy by Pieter Bregman/Fotolia.com | Rabbits by Joss/Fotolia.com | NSD courtesy NSD & Broadie & Shadow.
Pg. 24: Woods by Bob McMullen courtesy City of Cambridge Photo Galleries | Crocuses courtesy Vic Lomic | Tulips courtesy Vic Lomic | Man in flood courtesy of Kitchener-Waterloo Record Photographic Negative Collection, University of Waterloo Library | All weather icons by puruan/Shutterstock.com | Victoria Park Splash Pad courtesy City of Kitchener Photo Galleries.
Pg. 25: Fall forest by JMO | All weather icons by puruan/Shutterstock.com | Winter in Victoria Park courtesy of City of Kitchener Photo Galleries | Horse and Sled Waterloo Historical Society Collection accessed online http://vitacollections.ca/kpl-gsr/details.asp?ID=45043. | Christmas Light & Train courtesy City of Cambridge Photo Galleries.
Pg. 26: Globe accessed at http://pixabay.com/en/browser-internet-www-global-98386/ | Hespeler Library courtesy of City of Cambridge Photo Galleries | Canada Post, courtesy Canada Post Photo Centre | Old Post Office by Balcer accessed at http://commons.wikimedia.org/wiki/File:Old_Post_Office_Galt_Cambridge_Ontario.jpg (CC).
Pg. 27: New Hamburg Independent frontpage courtesy New Hamburg Independent | TV from Clikr accessed at http://www.clker.com/clipart-plasma-tv.html | Radio Microphone from Shutterstock.com | Rotary Phone from wikipedia by ProhibitOnions accessed at http://en.wikipedia.org/wiki/File:Model500Telephone1951.jpg.
Pg. 28: Otto Klotz by James Esson accessed at http://vitacollections.ca/kpl-gsr/details.asp?ID=44185, Waterloo Historical Society Collection | Grandview Public School courtesy Waterloo Region District School Board | Back to School by Lyudmyla Kharlamova/Shutterstock.com | Toddler with Glasses by Serhiy Kobyakov /Shutterstock.com | Students at Bluevale Collegiate courtesy Waterloo Region District School Board.
Pg. 29: Primary Class courtesy of Waterloo Catholic District School Board | School house image by JMO | St. Margaret School courtesy of Waterloo Catholic District School Board | Tutoring by Lisa F. Young/Shutterstock.com | French blocks by Jaimie Duplass/Shutterstock.com.
Pg. 30: Nurse by Bevan Goldswain/Shutterstock.com | Business Students by Dragon Images/Shutterstock.com | Doon Campus by David Bell accessed at http://en.wikipedia.org/wiki/File:Conestoga_College_Doon_Campus_Library_Pond_21-Oct-2012.jpg (CC) | What You Do courtesy of Conestoga College | Flowers with boots by Mariusz Szczygiel/Shutterstock.com.
Pg. 31: Esthetics training courtesy of Gina's college | Chocolate cake from Pixabay.com | Personal care worker by Monkey Business Images/Shutterstock.com | Lady on computer by Juan Nel/Shutterstock.com | Plumber by Minerva Studio/Shutterstock.com | Hardhat by Elnur/Shutterstock.com.
Pg. 32: Faculty of Music by Radagast accessed from http://en.wikipedia.org/wiki/File:LaurierU.jpg | Faculty of Social Work By permute accessed http://en.wikipedia.org/wiki/File:Wilfrid_Laurier_University,_Lyle_S._Hallman_Faculty_of_Social_Work,_Kitchener_Campus.jpg (CC) | Mike Morris courtesy Mike Morris and Sustainable Waterloo Region | WLU Lacrosse Team courtesy of Wilfrid Laurier University Archives and Special Collections | Business Notebook by pedrosek/Shutterstock.com | Piano by H.Kan/Shutterstock.com | Dedication of Seminary from Wilfred Laurier University Archives and Special Collections.
Pg. 33: Student Life Centre by Giligone at en.wikipedia accessed at http://en.wikipedia.org/wiki/File:Student_Life_Centre_Courtyard_at_the_University_of_Waterloo_in_August_2007.jpg (CC) | Engineering Building by Victor Vucicevich accessed at http://commons.wikimedia.org/wiki/File:University_of_Waterloo_Engineering_5_Bridge.jpg (CC) | Kevin O'Leary by Ontario Chamber of Commerce accessed at http://www.flickr.com/photos/ontariochamber/4171670649/ (CC) | Student by Bevan Goldswain/Shutterstock.com | Classroom courtesy University of Waterloo Archives.
Pg. 34: Cow by Dudarev Mikhail/Fotolia.com | Corn by atoss/Fotolia.com | Martin's courtesy Martin's Family Fruit Farm. | Farmer Plowing by David Hunsberger courtesy of Mennonite Archives of Ontario | Breton courtesy of Dare Foods | Bottling – source unknown.
Pg. 35: All terrain courtesy Ontario Drive and Gear | Toyota car courtesy Toyota Motor Manufacturing Canada Inc. | Le Roy Car photo provided by Waterloo Region Museum, Region of Waterloo | Office Desk courtesy Krug | Machinist accessed from http://images.OurOntario.ca/waterloo/30272/data.
Pg. 36: SunLife office by Giligone accessed at http://en.wikipedia.org/wiki/File:Sun-Life_Financial_headquarters_Waterloo_Ontario.JPG (CC) | Paper etc by Oleksiy Mark/Shutterstock.com | The Wealthy Barber courtesy David Chilton | Waterloo Mutual Fire Insurance accessed at http://images.OurOntario.ca/waterloo/29796/data | CIGI Atrium by Brandon.currie accessed at http://www.flickr.com/photos/cigi_media/6351765296/in/photostream (CC) | ATM courtesy NCR.
Pg. 37: FunworX courtesy Bingamens | Langdon Hall courtesy of Langdon Hall | Pizza by Fanfo/Shutterstock.com | Tailor Shop accessed at http://images.OurOntario.ca/waterloo/47825/data | Handyman by auremar/Shutterstock.com.
Pg. 38: Mike Lazaridis by texlad accessed at http://en.wikipedia.org/wiki/File:Mike_Lazaridis.jpg (CC) | Graduate by v.s.anandhakrishna/Shutterstock.com | Light bulb by jannoon028/Shutterstock.com | Patented by Arcady/Shutterstock.com | Communitech Hub courtesy of Communitech.
Pg. 39: Blackberry from Blackberry Media Gallery accessed at http://ca.blackberry.com/content/dam/bbCompany/Desktop/Global/Device/Q10/Q10_Black_Front.jpg | Google Screenshot from Google, Google and the Google logo are registered trademarks of Google Inc. used with permission | Satellite courtesy of Com Dev | Apps by Umberto Shtanzman/Shutterstock.com.
Pg. 40: Soccer field courtesy MUSCO | Golfing/Hee Young Park courtesy Manulife Financial LPGA Classic | Rob Ducey courtesy of Toronto Blue Jays Baseball Club | Football by Dan Thornberg/Shutterstock.com.
Pg. 41: Chicopee by JMO | Hockey Player by Valeriy Lebedev/Fotolia.com | Skating Poster courtesy Preston Figure Skating Club | Curling stone by Felix accessed at http://commons.wikimedia.org/wiki/File:Curling_stones_on_rink_with_visible_pebble.jpg (CC) | Kelly VanderBeek courtesy Kelly VanderBeek.
Pg. 42: Laurel Creek by aurinkosanoo accessd at http://www.flickr.com/photos/aurinkosanoo/6224246327/in/photostream/ (CC) | Victor Davis courtesy of Region of Waterloo Swim Club | Waterpolo Ball by chrisbrignell/Shutterstock.com | Canoe by Smileus/Shutterstock.com | Fisherman by Ljupco Smokovski/Shutterstock.com | Swimming by Andrey Bandurenko /Fotolia.com.
Pg. 43: Tennis Racket from C-You/Shutterstock.com | Community Centry by JMO | Sherry Delany courtesy Cambridge Sports Hall of Fame | Table Tennis by Sergey Skleznev/Shutterstock.com | Volleyball by MariusdeGraf/Shutterstock.com | Basketball Players by Alexander Raths/Shutterstock.com | Lenox Lewis from wikipedia by nikkon- accessed at http://en.wikipedia.org/wiki/File:Lenox_Lewis_2010.jpg.
Pg. 44: Homer Watson painting courtesy Homer Watson Gallery | Carl Ahrens painting image courtesy KW Art Gallery | Flowers drawing courtesy of Jane Buyers | Florence Carlyle painting accessed at http://www.ago.net/agoid2621 | Clay Sculpture from Alexey V Smirnov/Shutterstock.com | Button Factory by JMO.
Pg. 45: KW Symphony by Sean M. Puckett courtesy of KW Symphony | Danny Micheal by www.iliaphotography from wikipedia accessed at http://en.wikipedia.org/wiki/File:Danny-michel-studio.jpeg (CC) | Eric Traplin courtesy Eric Traplin | Steven Strongman by Matthew Barnes courtesy Steven Strongman | Jane Archibald courtesy IMG Artists | Music notes from Pavel K/Shutterstock.com | Waterloo Band accessed at http://images.OurOntario.ca/waterloo/30659/data.
Pg. 46: Jill Hennessy by gdcgraphics accessed at http://en.wikipedia.org/wiki/File:JillHennessyTIFFSept10.jpg (CC) | Mary Poppins courtesy of Drayton Entertainment | Masks from Pixabay.com | Registry Theatre courtesy Registry Theatre.
Pg. 47: Malcom Gladwell by bunnicula accessed at http://www.flickr.com/photos/bunnicula/3198772084/ (CC) | John B. Crozier courtesy of Waterloo Region Hall of Fame | Schmecks Appeal cover courtesy Random House | David Morrell image by Philkno Phil Konstantin accessed at http://commons.wikimedia.org/wiki/File:DavidMorrellByPhilKonstantin.jpg (CC) | Face outline by Nikitina Olga/Shutterstock.com | Pile of Letters by Anton Balazh/Shutterstock.com | Books by Kim Nguyen/Shutterstock.com.
Pg. 48: Woman exercising by Hugo Felix/Shutterstock.com | Sledding by Firma V/Shutterstock.com | Syringe by Lorelyn Medina/Shutterstock.com | Books in Computer by koya979/Shutterstock.com | Boy brushing teeth by Sergiy Bykhunenko/Shutterstock.com | Fresh Food by Serg64/Shutterstock.com | Lyle Hallman courtesy Lyle Hallman Foundation.
Pg. 49: Nurse and patient by Alexander Raths/Shutterstock.com | School of Pharmacy by JMO | Charles Miller Fisher courtesy Waterloo Region Hall of Fame.
Pg. 50: WR-map adjusted by JMO, plus icons by JMO, from pixabay.com and Shutterstock.om [hereafter Various Map Icons] | Duke of Cambridge from wikipedia accessed at http://en.wikipedia.org/wiki/File:George_2nd_Cambridge.png
Pg. 51: Jacob Hespeler courtesy of City of Cambridge Archives | Claudette Miller courtesy of City of Cambridge Archives | Hespeler building by courtesy City of Cambridge Photo Galleries | Flour Mill courtesy of R Kinzie, An Insider's Guide to Waterloo Region | Rivers courtesy City of Cambridge Photo Galleries | Galt Dowtown courtesy City of Cambridge Photo Galleries | Sheaves Tower by JMO | Butterfly courtesy Cambridge Butterfly Conservatory | Mill Race festival by Justin Bastin courtesy Mill Race Festival.

Pg. 52: WR-map adjusted by JMO and Various Map Icons | Lord Kitchener accessed at http://en.wikipedia.org/wiki/File:Kitchener-Britons.jpg.

Pg. 53: MacKenzie King by Topley Studio, Library and Archives Canada,PA-027003 | Lisa LaFlemme courtesy CTV | Rockway by JMO | City Hall from wikipedia accessed at http://en.wikipedia.org/wiki/File:Kitchener-city-hall.jpg (CC)| Splash park courtesy of Bingamens | Woodside by JMO | Centre in the Square courtesy City of Kitchener Photo Galleries | Cityscape courtesy Matthew Smith | Cruising on King courtesy City of Kitchener Photo Galleries.

Pg. 54: WR-map adjusted by JMO and Various Map Icons | Battle of Waterloo by William Sadler II accessed at http://en.wikipedia.org/wiki/File:Battle_of_Waterloo_1815.PNG.

Pg. 55: Moses Springer accessed at http://images.ourontario.ca/waterloo/29701/image/80451 | Gerald Hagey accessed at http://images.ourontario.ca/Laurier/44500/image/83167?n=2 Laurier University photograph collection | RIM park by JMO | Erb house by JMO | Dinosaurs courtesy University of Waterloo Earth Science Museum | Perimeter Institute by JMO | Clay & Glass Gallery image of Tactile Desires: The Work of Jack Sure; Curators: Timothy Long, MacKenzie Art Gallery & Virginia Eichhorn, Tom Thomson Art Gallery courtesy Clay & Glass Gallery | Uptown Waterloo by Area256 accessed http://en.wikipedia.org/wiki/File:Uptown_Waterloo,_Ontario.jpg (CC).

Pg. 56: WR-map adjusted by JMO and Various Map Icons | MidleSteeple, Dumfries by MSDMSD accessed at http://en.wikipedia.org/wiki/File:Midsteeple,_Dumfries_2010.JPG (CC).

Pg. 57: John Goldie courtesy Waterloo Hall of Fame | Daniel B. Detweiler courtesy Waterloo Region Hall of Fame | Centennial Park courtesy North Dumfries Township | Meeting House by JMO | Aggregate by JMO | Frozen Pond courtesy North Dumfries Township | Centre Building courtesy North Dumfries Township | Plowing courtesy International Plowing Match Expo | Road courtesy North Dumfries Township | Rubber Duck by AlexanderKlink accessed at http://commons.wikimedia.org/wiki/File:Rubber_Duck.jpg isolated by JM0 (CC).

Pg. 58: WR-map adjusted by JMO and Various Map Icons | Richard Colley Wellesley by Thomas Lawrence accessed at http://en.wikipedia.org/wiki/File:Richard_Wellesley.jpeg.

Pg. 59: Deborah Glaister courtesy Wellesley Historical Society | David Johnston by Valacosa accessed at http://en.wikipedia.org/wiki/File:David_Lloyd_Johnston(Brubacher_House).jpg (CC) | Church by JMO | Historic Building by JMO | Wellesley Township Hall by JMO | Paradise Lake courtesy YMCAs of Cambridge & Kitchener-Waterloo | Farm by JMO | Cheese by Hong Vo/Shutterstock.com | Apples by Brzostowska/Shutterstock.com | Parade courtesy Wellesley Historical Society.

Pg. 60: WR-map adjusted by JMO and Various Map Icons | Sir Wilmot-Horton by R.J. Lane accessed at http://en.wikipedia.org/wiki/File:SirRobertWilmotHorton.jpg.

Pg. 61: Sir Adam Beck photo courtesy of Hydro One Networks Inc, reprinted with permission | Elsie Cressman courtesy KW Negative Collection | Water Wheel courtesy Lynn B. | Castle Kilbride courtesy of Castle Kilbride National Historic Site | Sunfish Lake by Kevin Thompson accessed at http://en.wikipedia.org/wiki/File:Sunfish_Sunshine_copy.jpg (CC) | Oasis park by JMO | Baden Hills courtesy R Kinzie, An Insider's Guide to Waterloo Region | Strawberries by tinnko/Shutterstock.com | Quilt by GG/Fotolia.com.

Pg. 62: WR-map adjusted by JMO and Various Map Icons | Royal Arsenal Gatehouse by Fin Fahey accessed at http://en.wikipedia.org/wiki/File:Woolwich_royal_arsenal_gatehouse_1.jpg (CC).

Pg. 63: Ken Seiling courtesy Region of Waterloo accessed at http://www.regionofwaterloo.ca/en/regionalGovernment/resources/Ken%20Seiling%20Web%20pic.jpg | Darryl Sittler courtesy Kitchener-Waterloo Record Photographic Negative Collection | Memorial Centre by Saskia2586 accessed at http://en.wikipedia.org/wiki/File:Woolwich_Mem_Centre.jpg (GNU) | Kissing Bridge by Optionbooter accessed at http://en.wikipedia.org/wiki/File:Kissing_Bridge_David_Sullivan.jpg (CC) | Horse and buggy by Saskia2586 accessed at http://en.wikipedia.org/wiki/File:Menno_Horse.jpg (GNU) | St. Jacobs Farmers' Market by Saskia2586 accessed at http://en.wikipedia.org/wiki/File:St_Jacobs_Farmers_Market.jpg(GNU) | Merry-Hill Golf Course courtesy Merry Hill Golf Course | Number One by Arcady/Shutterstock.com | Pancakes by Hurst Photo/Shuterstock.com | Festival image courtesy R. Kinzie, An Insider's Guide to Waterloo Region.

Pg. 64: Gear by Lightspring/Shutterstock.com | Car by Alexkava/Shutterstock.com | Cover from 100 Years of Progress in Waterloo County Canada, Chronicle-Telegraph photo by JMO | Businessman by Samuel Borges Photography/Shutterstock.com | Business Growth by RAJ CREATIONZS/Shutterstock.com.

Pg. 65: Uptown by Gilgone from Wikipedia from http://en.wikipedia.org/wiki/File:Uptown_Waterloo_Ontario.JPG (CC) | Sign by Dirk Ercken/Shutterstock | Farm by JMO | Museum photo provided by Waterloo Region Museum, Region of Waterloo | Blue Box by Elena Elisseeva/Shutterstock.com | Bandages by Lim Yong Hian/Shutterstock.com | Glass by Palo_ok/Shutterstock.com.

Pg. 66: Helping Hand by C Jones/Shutterstock.com | Random Act courtesy The Kitchener and Waterloo Community Foundation | Senior by Melpomene/Shutterstock.com | Teamwork by america365/Shutterstock.com | Light Bulb by Sujono by sujono/Shutterstock.com | Drinking Milk by Serhiy Kobyakov/Shutterstock.com | Food Box by Steve Cukrov/Fotolia.com | Barnraising courtesy Mennonite Archives of Ontario.

Pg. 67: Balloons by snake3d/Shutterstock.com | Stars by timquo/Shutterstock.com | Snowman by ekler/Shutterstock.com | Flag by gualtiero boffi/Shutterstock.com | Oktoberfest Trumpeters courtesy KW Oktoberfest | Saengerfest accessed at http://images.ourontario.ca/Partners/Waterloo/WatPL29670f.jpg | The Record courtesy Waterloo Region Record.

Pg. 68: Toronto by Gheorghe Roman/Fotolia.com | Giraffe by jaroslava V/Shutterstock.com | Snowboarder by gillmar/Shutterstock.com | Mary Stuart Production photo by David Hou courtesy Stratford Festival | Lake Huron by Brian Lasenby/Shutterstock.com.

Pg. 69: Atom from pixabay.com | Train & Apartment by JMO | Possible by Ivelin Radkov/Shutterstock | Child reading by Samuel Borges Photography/Shutterstock.com | Teamwork by Ivelin Radkov/Shutterstock.com | Maple Tree by Le Do/Shutterstock.com.

Pg. 71: Kitchener at night courtesy Matthew Smith.

Pg. 72: City Hall by Illustratedjc accessed at http://en.wikipedia.org/wiki/File:KitchenerCityHall.JPG (CC).

## Bibliography

General resources used are listed below. For specific facts or quotations cited, see the Endnotes section.


Boomfield, Elizabeth (1995) *Waterloo Township Through Two Centuries.* Waterloo, Ont: Waterloo Historical Society, c1995 (hereafter, WTTTC).

City of Cambridge (Accessed 2013) City of Cambridge website, http://www.cambridge.ca/ (hereafter Web:C.C).

City of Kitchener (Accessed 2013) City of Kitchener website, http://www.kitchener.ca/en/ (hereafter Web:C.K).

City of Waterloo (Accessed 2013) City of Waterloo website, http://www.waterloo.ca/ (hereafter Web: C.W).

Concordia Club (Accessed 2013) Concordia Club website, http:///www.concordiaclub.ca/ (hereafter Web:C.Club).

Eby, Ezra (1895 and 1896) *A Biographical History of Early Settlers and Their Descendants in Waterloo Township* accessed at http://ebybook.region.waterloo.on.ca/ (hereafter Eby Book).

Hayes, Geoffrey William (1997) *Waterloo County: An Illustrated History*. Kitchener, Ont: Waterloo Historical Society, 1997 (hereafter WC: AIH).

Kearney, Mark and Ray, Randy (2000) *The Ontario Fact Book*. Whitecap Books, 2000 (hereafter TOFB).

McLaughlin, Kenneth (1987) *Cambridge: The Making of a Canadian City.* Burlington, Ont.: Windsor Publications (Canada) Ltd., (hereafter CTMCC).

McLaughlin, Kenneth and Fleuren, Kristel (2000) *Hespeler: Portrait of an Ontario Town.* Waterloo, ON (hereafter HPOT).

Moyer, Bill (1970) *Bill Moyer's Waterloo Country Diary*. CHYM, Kitchener, ON.

Moyer, Bill (1971) *This Unique Heritage : The Story of Waterloo County*. CHYM, Kitchener, ON (hereafter TUH).

Region of Waterloo (Accessed 2013) Region of Waterloo website, http://www.regionofwaterloo.ca/en/ (hereafter Web: RofW).

Statistics Canada (Accessed 2013) Statistics Canada website, http://www.statcan.gc.ca/start-debut-eng.html (hereafter Web:SC).

Township of North Dumfries (Accessed 2013) Township of North Dumfries website, http://www.northdumfries.ca/en/ (hereafter Web:TofND).

Township of Wellesely (Accessed 2013) Township of Wellesely website, http://www.township.wellesley.on.ca/ (hereafter Web: TofWE).

Township of Wilmot (Accessed 2013) Township of Wilmot website, http://www.wilmot.ca/ (hereafter Web:TofWI).

Township of Woolwich (Accessed 2013) Township of Woolwich website, http://www.woolwich.ca/en/ (hereafter Web:TofWO).

Waterloo Region Museum (Accessed 2013) Waterloo Region Museum website, http://waterlooregionmuseum.com/ (hereafter Web:WRM).


## End Notes

Pg. 4: [1] Statistics Canada, Census Profile, Regional Municipality of Waterloo, 2011 (hereafter Stats Can. WR) | [2] Statistics Canada, NHS Focus on Geography Series, 2011 for each city and township listed in table at Web: SC.

Pg. 5: [1, 2] Current population estimates, Report: P-13-023 "Year End 2012 Population and Household Estimates for the Region of Waterloo" Region of Waterloo (hereafter RofW Population Estimate) | [3,4] Historical populations, WC: AIH, (including Appendix 1). Also, Waterloo Region was know as Waterloo Township and/or Waterloo County during much of this time. | [5] Future population estimate: Report P12-054 "Year End 2011 Population and Household Estimates" Region of Waterloo | [6] Region of Waterloo, Census Bulletin, Population and Dwelling Counts, Statistics from the 2011 Census for Waterloo Region.

Pg. 6: [1] Educational program at Rare Charitable Research Reserve.

Pg. 8: [1] WCD, pg 20.

Pg. 10: [1] Web:WRM — Waterloo Region Hall of Fame.

Pg. 11: [1] Web:WRM — Waterloo Region Hall of Fame.

Pg. 12: [1] Web:WRM — Waterloo Region Hall of Fame | [2] http://www.lib.uwaterloo.ca/discipline/SpecColl/archives/LangTanning.html.

Pg. 13: [1] Web:C.Club | [2] TOFB.

Pg. 14: [1] CTMCC.

Pg. 16: [1-3] NHS Focus on Geography Series - Kitchener - Cambridge - Waterloo, Analytical products, 2011 | [4-6] Stats Can. WR.

Pg. 17: [1-6] Stats Can. WR.

Pg. 18: [1] Stats Can. WR.

Pg. 19: [1,7] Stats Can. WR | [2] Average home price, Solid Home Sales in October (2013), KW Associatiion of Realators accessed at http://www.kwar.ca/solid-homes-sales-in-october/ | [3] Eby Book | [4] http://www.reincanada.com/RealEstateNewsView/tabid/72/articleType/ArticleView/articleId/100/Ontarios-Top-Investment-Towns-Named-For-2009-2014.aspx | [5-6] Canada Mortgage and Housing Corporation, Rental Market Report, Fall 2012.

Pg. 20: [1-2] Web:RofW | [3] http://www.grt.ca/en/aboutus/fastfacts.asp | [4] http://images.OurOntario.ca/waterloo/29704/data.

Pg. 23: [1] http://www.nsd.on.ca/ | [2] TUH.

Pg. 24: [1-4] Canadian Climate Normals 1971-2000, Environment Canada (hereafter CCN).

Pg. 25: [1-6] CCN.

Pg. 26: [1] http://www.cambridgelibraries.ca/about/history.

Pg. 27: [1] WTTTC, pg 326 | [2] http://www.intelligentwaterloo.com/en/index.shtml.

Pg. 28: [1] Web:WRM -- Waterloo Region Hall of Fame | [2-7] WRDSB, http://www.wrdsb.ca/ (for all WRDSB data) | [8] WC: AIH, pg 72.

Pg. 29: [1-4] WCDSB, http://www.wcdsb.ca/ (for all WCDSB data).

Pg. 30: [1-4] Conestoga College, http://www.conestogac.on.ca/.

Pg 31: [1] http://www.ginascollege.com/ | [2] http://www.liaisoncollege.com/ | [3] http://www.trios.com/ | [4] http://www.medixcollege.ca/.

Pg. 32: [1] WLU, http://www.wlu.ca/.

Pg. 33: [1-7] Universtiy of Waterloo, http://uwaterloo.ca/.

Pg. 34: [1-4] Region of Waterloo Census Bulletin, 2011 Census #2, Agriculture | [5] http://www.darefoods.com.

Pg. 35: [1] http://www.tmmc.ca |[2] http://images.OurOntario.ca/waterloo/30272/data.

Pg. 36: [1] Statistics Canada, NHS Profile, Waterloo, RM, Ontario, 2011, Web: Stats Can. | [2] http://sunlife.ca | [3] http://images.OurOntario.ca/waterloo/29796/data.

Pg. 37: [1] http://www.walper.com/the_hotel.html | [2] http://www.langdonhall.ca/Awards-and-Accolades | [3] http://images.OurOntario.ca/waterloo/47825/data.

Pg. 39: [1-2] https://www.communitech.ca/ | [2] http://kik.com/.

Pg. 47: [1] Web:WRM -- Waterloo Region Hall of Fame | [2] http://oboc.ca.

Pg. 48: [1] http://chd.region.waterloo.on.ca/.

Pg. 50: [1-2] RofW Population Estimate | [3-5] Statistics Canada, NHS Focus on Geography Series, 2011, Cambridge, Web:SC | [6] RofW Population Estimate (Cambridge) divided by Census (Cambridge) land size estimate | [7-9] Web: C.C (for general amenities).

Pg. 52: [1-2] RofW Population Estimate | [3-5] Statistics Canada, NHS Focus on Geography Series, 2011, Kitchener, Web:SC | [6] RofW Population Estimate (Kitchener) divided by Census (Kitchener) land size estimate | [7-8] Web: C.K. (for general employment and community amenities).

Pg. 54: [1] Intelligent community from http://www.intelligentwaterloo.com/en/ | [2-3] RofW Population Estimate | [4-6] Statistics Canada, NHS Focus on Geography Series, 2011, Waterloo, Web:SC | [7] RofW Population (Waterloo) Estimate divided by Census (Waterloo) land size estimate | [8-9] Web:C.W (general employment and amenities).

Pg. 56: [1-2] RofW Population Estimate | [3-5] Statistics Canada, NHS Focus on Geography Series, 2011, North Dumfries Township, Web:SC | [6] RofW Population (North Dumfries) estimate divided by Census: (North Dumfries) land size estimate | [7-8] Web:TofND (general employment and amenities).

Pg. 58: [1, 4-6] Statistics Canada, NHS Focus on Geography Series, 2011, Township of Wellesley, Web:SC | [2-3] RofW Population Estimate | [7] RofW Population (Wellesley) estimate divided by Census (Wellesley) land size estimate | [8-9] Web:Tof WE (general employment and amenities).

Pg. 60: [1,7] RofW Population (Wilmot) estimate divided by Census (Wilmot) land size estimate | [2-3] RofW Population Estimate | [4-6] Statistics Canada, NHS Focus on Geography Series, 2011, Township of Wilmot, Web:SC | [8-9] Web:TofWI (general employment and amenities) | [10] Statistics Canada, Census Profile, New Hamburg 2011.

Pg. 62: [1-2] RofW Population Estimate | [3-5] Statistics Canada, NHS Focus on Geography Series, 2011, Township of Woolwich Web:SC | [6] RofW Population (Woolwich) estimate divided by Census (Woolwich) land size estimate | [7-8] Web:TofWO (general employment and amenities) | [9] Statistics Canada, Census Profile, Elmira, 2011 | [10] Statistics Canada, Census Profile, St. Jacobs, 2011.

Pg. 63: [1] http://www.elmiramaplesyrup.com/.

Pg. 64 [1-3] Census Bulletin Place of Work and Commuting to Work, Region of Waterloo, Planning Housing and Community Services, Statistics from the 2006 census | [4] Quick Facts (2013) Canada's Technology Triangle.

Pg. 65: [1] http://www.regionofwaterloo.ca/en/regionalgovernment/visionmissionvalues.asp | [2] Web:RofW | [3-4] Web:WRM.

CPSIA information can be obtained at www.ICGtesting.com
Printed in the USA
LVIW01n1648260615
444045LV00001B/1